THE HENDRIX EXPERIENCE

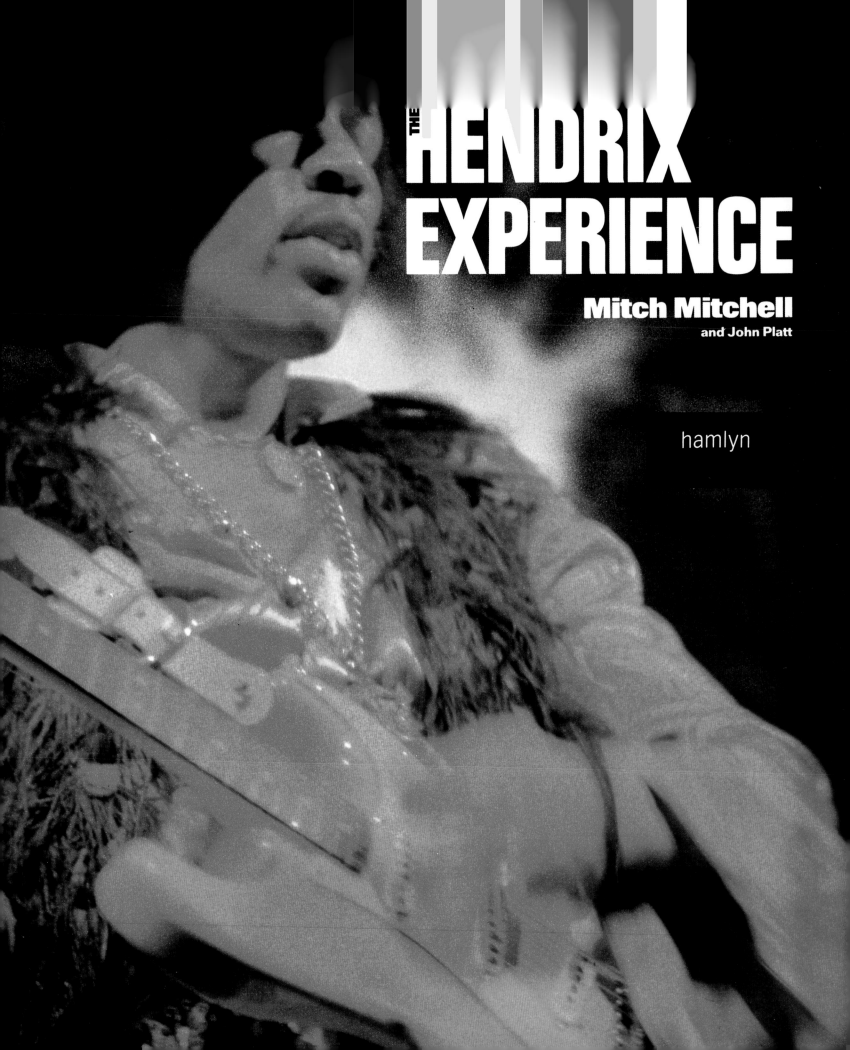

THE HENDRIX EXPERIENCE

Mitch Mitchell

and John Platt

hamlyn

Acknowledgements

Mitch Mitchell would like to thank Colin Newman; Prab Nallamilli, Gary Davies of, and Nick Wiszowaty, PR man for London's Hard Rock Café; Piers Murray Hill (Publisher), David Heslam (Editor), Leigh Jones (Designer), Julia Pashley (Picture Researcher) and Russell Porter (Jacket Designer) of Paul Hamlyn Publishing; Johnathan Crystal LL.B. (Hons) Barrister-at-Law; Ken Voss of The Jimi Hendrix Information Management Institute, Des Plaines, Illinois, USA; Margaret Redding; Martin and Cath Kingston of The Kilty Stone, Clonakilty, Southern Ireland; The Shanley Family of Shanley's, Clonakilty, Southern Ireland – in fact all the people of Clonakilty, who showed us such great kindness and friendship; and, of course, Dee, the old boot, who worked above and beyond the call of duty on this book.

John Platt would like to thank Eva Hunte (for keeping me sane whilst writing and researching); Ken Mitchell (for answering some really difficult queries); Yves at Vinyl Solution (for loan of the record sleeves), John at Kall Kwik in Chiswick; Peter Doggett and Mark Paytress at Record Collector and Mark Heyward at Vinyl Experience.

Mitch Mitchell would also like to thank the following for their quick and accurate help in compiling and checking the appearances itinerary:

Europe: Sophie Gallovedec, Joel De Vouges, Lysette de Veltre and the great Johnny Halliday – France; Arturo Bonnacci – Italy; Lottie Vollmer – Germany; Sveriges TV and the staff at Grona Lund – Sweden; Gerry T. Walker – Holland; Annabel Fielding, Musidisc, U.K., The British Library, Melody Maker Magazine, BBC TV and Radio, Robert Wyatt, Hugh Hopper, Phyl Mitchell, Joyce Goodman, Errol Fuller, The French Embassy in London, Kensington and Chelsea Library – U.K.; Helena Kaukenon, Mr Haarma, Helsinki TV, Sanomat Newspaper – Finland. U.S.A. and Canada: Maurice Wheeler, Detroit Public Library, Azalia Hackley Section; Jeannie Morrell, New York; Variety Magazine; Billboard; Mary Cullen, Cleveland and Chicago; Linda Peters, Augusta, Georgia; Kathryn Ray, Martin Luther King Memorial Library, Washington DC; Dick Clarke Productions, Los Angeles; Columbia Pictures; San Francisco Chronicle; Sally Ann Davis, Houston, Texas; Ken Voss, Illinois; Nancy McNeil, Toronto, Canada.

Photographic Acknowlededgments

The publishers wish to thank the following photographers and organisations for their kind permission to reproduce their photographs in this publication:

Aquarius Picture Library 7, 87; Art Rock left; Associated Press 77 top; Chuck Boyd/Flower Children Ltd 117, 122, 123; Brian Bradbury 145; Camera Press 30, 36 bottom,/Paul Anthony 148; Josh Ellis 167 top right; Bill Graham 1968, #105 Artist Rick Griffin 62 right, 110 right,/#140 Victor Moscoso 119; Nona Hatay 133, 134, 135, 138, 159, 168; Jimi Hendrix Information Management Institute and Kenneth Voss 154,/Nancy Diedrich 116,/Allan Koss 99, 141, 144-145, 150-151,/George Shuba 136,/Craig Soloman 128,/Dave Sygall 103 bottom; Jean-Pierre Leloir 12, 28, 44 right, 45, 54, 55, 73 bottom, 75, 76, 108, 109, 157; London Features International 35 bottom, 47, 51 inset, 113, 121, 129 bottom, 137,/Frontline 31,/Michael Ochs Archive 58, 161,/SKR 23; Linda McCartney 64, 65, 66, 67, 69, 104, 105, 106, 107, 110 left, 11; Mitch Mitchell Collection 10, 11 top, 11 bottom, 13, 14, 16 top, 19, 68, 70, 71, 93, 94, 95, 102, 127 left, 129 top, 139 top left, 142, 143 left, 146 bottom, 147 top, 147 bottom left, 147 bottom right, 165 top, 166 top; Mrs Phyl Mitchell 33, 48 inset; Monitor Syndication 9; Osiris Visions Ltd 63 right; Pictorial Press Ltd 17, 20, 21, 24, 25, 26-27, 29, 32, 36 top, 39, 41, 42, 43 right, 46, 48, 51, 60, 73, top, 77, 81, 89 left, 97, 100, 114-115, 120-121, 139 top right, 149, 158, 163, 164, bottom; John Platt Collection 59, 165 bottom; Polydor Ltd 78, 98, 103 top, 146 top, 162; Popperfoto 35 top left, 43 left, 44 left, 72, 84, 87 insert; David Redfern 18,/Elliot Landy titlepage; Relay Photos 16 bottom, 22 left, 89 right; Rex Features Ltd 40, 52, 53, 56, 61, 80, 130; Eathan A Russel 82; Scope Features 74; Barrie Wentzell 124, 125, 126 right, 127 right, 155, 156; Val Wilmer 85, 167 top left.

Every effort has been made by the publishers to credit organisations and individuals with regard to the supply of photographs and illustrations. the publishers apologise for any omissions arising from their inability to trace the original artists and photographers.

First published in 1990
This edition published in 2000 by Hamlyn, an imprint of
Octopus Publishing Group Limited,
2-4 Heron Quays, London E14 4JP

A Catalogue record for this book is available from the British Library
ISBN 0 600 59538 2
Copyright © Mitch Mitchell and John Platt 1990
Copyright © 1990, 2000 Octopus Publishing Group Limited
Appearances itinerary © Mitch Mitchell

Printed and bound in China

CONTENTS

DEDICATION

There are very few musicians who are given the chance of working with someone as unique as Jimi. He gave me the space, time, encouragement and inspiration – I was so lucky. I miss my friend as much today as ever.

So this book is dedicated with love, not only to my mum and dad (Phyl and Jack), who were always there for me, but to **JAMES MARSHALL HENDRIX**. Hope this sets *some* of the record straight, mate.

Mitch Mitchell
London, England 1990

NO EXPERIENCE NECESSARY

O N SEPTEMBER 23 1966 JIMI HENDRIX ARRIVED in London accompanied by the ex-Animals bass guitarist, Chas Chandler. To a passerby Hendrix must have cut a somewhat comic figure – a man with wild, hair dressed in a conservative Burberry raincoat. But what he was wearing was just about all he possessed, his other clothes having been used to pay his hotel bill in New York.

Jimi had been earning in New York, but not enough, and his talent had gone generally unrecognized by those who mattered in the music business. He was in London to put that right and Chandler, newly entered into management, was going to help him.

The story of how Jimi Hendrix was discovered is now well known. After several years of work on the Southern 'chitlin' circuit' playing guitar back-up in several bands, some famous, some less so, he settled in New York in 1965. While still continuing to tour, he hooked up with Curtis Knight, whose band, the Squires, played regularly in and around New York. Still frustrated, Hendrix moved down to the predominantly white, but undoubtedly bohemian and tolerant surroundings of Greenwich Village. Although he continued to play behind other people, such as John Hammond Jnr, he started forming his own bands, known variously as Jimmy James and the Blue Flames and Rain Flower. Greenwich Village was awash with clubs of all persuasions,

jazz clubs, blues clubs, folk clubs – some quite upmarket, most less so. It was in one of the sleazier places, the Cafe Wha!, that the band got its first proper gigs. It was there that he was spotted by an English girl, Linda Keith, who, totally mesmerized by his performance, took to pestering her English rock-star friends to check out Hendrix. Her primary target was Chas Chandler. Two days later, on September 3, Chandler saw Hendrix and couldn't believe that he had not yet been signed up. He offered to take Hendrix over to England, fix him up with English musicians and a record contract and generally manage his career (in conjunction, as it turned out, with Chandler's own manager Mike Jeffery).

The days that followed Jimi's arrival in London saw Chandler introducing him to fellow musicians, taking him to various clubs, and setting up situations for Jimi to play. They also started holding auditions for what was to become The Experience. Noel Redding, despite the fact that he had never played bass before, got the job after only two auditions. The position of drummer proved more problematical.

Amongst the several drummers auditioned was John 'Mitch' Mitchell who had just left the soul-influenced Georgie Fame and the Blue Flames – rather sooner than he had intended. ·

Mitch, a Londoner by birth, had just turned twenty but already he had a wealth of 'showbiz'

*Jimi: Head full of ideas
'66.*

Chandler saw Hendrix and couldn't believe that he had not yet been signed up.

*Mitch at 13 drumming
with Pete Nelson and
The Travellers (Note Vic
Briggs on the right!)*

experience to look back on. Early on his parents had recognized a talent for entertaining others and, at the age of ten, had enrolled him in a theatrical school. Soon he was appearing in radio plays and singing advertising jingles and by his 12th birthday had achieved a modest fame as the hero of the BBC TV children's series 'Jennings'.

By this time, however, Mitch had discovered a greater love than acting – music. Through his advertising work he had come into contact with musicians and recording studios and he was soon hooked on the drums which he had always shown a natural affinity for. More TV work followed 'Jennings' but, by his 14th birthday, it was taking second place to music. He took a job in Jim Marshall's Hanwell guitar shop (of Marshall Amp fame) and soon began to pick up gigs through the musicians that called by.

Evening classes were neglected as he gained experience with local bands such as Pete Nelson and The Travellers who featured, amongst others, Vic Briggs the guitarist, who later on joined Eric Burdon and The Animals. The Coronets provided him with his first experience of a foreign tour, Germany, and some of the earliest session work took place with Ray Davies of The Kinks. But perhaps Mitch's most significant early musical experience occurred one night waiting for a bus outside The Ealing Club.

I remember hearing – no feeling – this rumble like thunder coming up through the paving stones. I went to check it out and discovered Graham Bond's Organization that is, Jack Bruce, Ginger Baker and Graham Bond. This was the first time I realized how powerful a trio could feel – I don't mean volume but intensity. I believe it was the first time Jack played electric bass, borrowed because he broke a string on his upright.

B Y 1965 HE HAD JOINED HIS FIRST FULL-TIME band, The Riot Squad, and was being increasingly recognized as one of (if not *the*) best rock session drummers in the UK.

I worked with the Les Reed Orchestra, who did Ready Steady Go! when it was done live in Wembley. Doing RSG! with them was my

ABOVE:
Mitch in 1958 as Jennings in the BBC TV series, 'Jennings at School'.

LEFT:
1956 – Mitch stuck to drums after this.

first major session. I also did several sessions with Tony Hatch, a few with Petula Clark, Joe Meek, Brenda Lee, loads of different people. I got a lot of sessions because I was a rock drummer – a lot of the older guys or the jazz musicians couldn't cut it for the pop stuff – even though I couldn't read very well. After a while, however, I got to recognize the triplets. I was lucky because the other young studio players coming up were the likes of Jimmy Page and Johnny Baldwin (John Paul Jones). Even then they were powerful players. I always felt envious that it was just a guitar and amp in hand for them while I had to cart around all my drums.

Around the time that I was leaving The Riot Squad I was hired by Radio Caroline and Seltaeb, The Beatles merchandising company, as a kind of talent scout, for about six weeks. They paid me £30 a week and I could still do all the sessions I wanted. If I saw anybody I thought was good I just had to let them know. The only person I suggested was someone I'd seen long before in a London folk club. They turned my suggestion down. It was a bloke named Paul Simon.

MITCH'S GROWING REPUTATION LED TO AN approach from Georgie Fame who was looking to replace his drummer. The Blue Flames, who had had a UK no. 1 ('Yeh Yeh' in January 1965), were several cuts above The Riot Squad and an important part of Mitch's musical education.

Through playing with these musicians I got to hear Thelonius Monk, Coltrane and Oliver Nelson. Drummers like Max Roach,

Elvin Jones, Philly Joe Jones and, of course, Tony Williams, changed my life. I already loved and stole from Earl Palmer, Benny Benjamin and Al Jackson. I still do, who doesn't?

IT WAS PROBABLY THE BEST ALL-ROUND MUSICAL education a young player could have had in the UK at that time. One fateful day, though, the following October, the band were called into the office and, although he didn't realize it, Mitch's life was about to change – somewhat considerably.

OPPOSITE PAGE:
One of our first gigs in France. 'The Olympia', Paris, 1966.

LEFT:
Chas Chandler. New York, 1967.

I was lucky because the other young studio players coming up were the likes of Jimmy Page and Johnny Baldwin (John Paul Jones). Even then they were powerful players. I always felt envious that it was just a guitar and amp in hand for them while I had to cart around all my drums.

Mitch (A.K.A. John Mitchell) Georgie Fame and The Blue Flames. London 1966.

I'd been working with Georgie Fame And The Blue Flames for 18 months. Every Monday the band went in and got its pay cheque and this particular Monday we all went in and were all fired. Every band that worked for the Rik Gunnell organization, from John Mayall to Zoot Money, went in on a Monday to be paid. On this occasion it was 'Lads, come into the office!' We went in one by one and it was, 'Sorry, but the band's being folded and you're fired.'

I was quite devastated and being the last one to join the band, my pay-off was quite small.

I went back home to my folks' place in Ealing, where I was still living and the next day I got a call from Chas Chandler. He told me he had this artist he'd just brought over from America. Was I interested in having a play?

I said, 'What does it entail?'

He said, 'All we've got is two weeks' work in France, with Johnny Halliday!'

So I said, 'What's the deal?'

'Best you come along and have a play!'

I made a few phone calls around and it turned out they'd auditioned every bloody drummer in England, near enough, including a lot of people I knew. The one thing that was really surprising to me was that in such a small place as London with the grapevine as it was at that time, you'd generally hear of what was going on. I hadn't heard a word about this guy and he'd been in the country a couple of weeks up to that point. He'd played with Cream and Zoot Money and people that I knew and it really fazed me.

The drummers they'd auditioned, who were mates of mine, hadn't mentioned anything to me. Mind you, not being blasé about it, if I had heard something in the weeks before, would I have done anything about it? I was still with Georgie Fame, not on a wage but getting paid by the gig, doing quite a lot for an 18–19-year-old kid. It would have been difficult to pass up, say £120 a week average, and go – as it turned out – to basically nothing.

At the audition it was strange. I met this black guy with very, very wild hair wearing this Burberry raincoat. He looked very straight really, apart from the hair. We didn't talk much at first – you've got to remember this was an audition for me sandwiched in between two sessions. Jimi was very soft-spoken and gave the impression of being very gentle, almost shy. It was immediately apparent that he was a good guitarist; but at that stage I was more knocked out that he could cover so many different styles as well. You name it he could do it. I think we did 'Have Mercy Babe' first. Jimi didn't really sing, more mumbled along to the music – Chas really had to coax it out of him. But we both clearly loved the same types of music.

So there we were in this tiny basement club, playing with these ridiculously small amps and for about two hours we ran through what we all knew – your Chuck Berry roots, Wilson Pickett, basically R&B stuff that everyone knows and accepts. Just feeling each other out.

I didn't know then that Noel had only just picked up a bass for the first time. Apparently he got the gig because he had the right haircut – but them's the breaks, you know? I remember throwing a few things at Hendrix. I really like Curtis Mayfield and The Impressions and I was astounded that he knew that style really, really fluently. He wasn't that flash as a guitarist on that occasion, it was more just going over rhythmic structures. I suppose we got through a lot of material in the two hours, but I got a little pissed off because I didn't really know how Jimi wanted me to play.

I said, 'Well, do you want me to play like Ginger Baker?' but I had no idea that Jimi wanted a kind of three piece situation, like Cream, at that stage. Nor I think did the management. The idea was for Hendrix to come over and front not exactly a soul review, but for them to put together a complete backing unit for him, and why not? I was fortunate that he didn't feel that way. In fact, I'm not sure that Jimi knew exactly what he wanted, that didn't come until we rehearsed properly the following week.

After that initial session, I think it was only a few hours later that I got a call from Chas saying, 'Yes, we're interested, would you like to have another play?' and I said, 'Well, quite honestly, what is the deal?'

'We've got the two weeks' work and that's all I can offer you at this point. I can give you twenty quid a week!'

I didn't exactly leap straight at it, 'Well, the two weeks' work sounds great. The only stipulation is that I don't work for a wage. I'll muck in for the two weeks but we'll work it out after that.'

I didn't know Chas Chandler very well at that point. I'd seen him working with The

ABOVE:
Jimi. Early days in London. 1966.

Animals, obviously, as The Blue Flames and The Animals had done several gigs together, but it was just like a nodding acquaintance. I didn't know that he'd given up playing completely, but he obviously had great faith in Hendrix. He'd sold his bass to finance Jimi, and that sort of thing.

The second or third time that we played, things started to stretch out considerably. That's when I started to feel it was a real chance, having come from such a structured unit as The Blue Flames, with horns and very tight arrangements, to come to something as loose as Hendrix. To have that much freedom was like being released from

Left:
Mitch with 'The Riot Squad'. London 1964.

Below Right:
One of our first English T.V. Shows 'Top Of The Pops' early '67.

Hendrix said 'Well, we've got some gigs coming up, let's do "Midnight Hour".' I, being a cocky little bastard at the time said, 'Oh fuck! Not this again. I've just come from doing "Midnight Hour" for two years. We've got a new band, can't we do better than this? Please?'

prison, and to have another musician prepared to give you that freedom was a most fortunate thing. I'd been lucky to play in The Blue Flames who had other, older musicians like Cliff Barton and Glen Hughes, who turned me on to people like Coltrane and Mingus. Maybe that background gave me the idea to attempt to play some of the things I'd heard.

In terms of our respective roles, don't forget that Noel had only just picked up the bass. Burns, the guitar company, had lent him a six-string bass, and he was still very guitar-orientated, not surprisingly. Hendrix had a definite feel for how a bass part should be, but really he was as easy-going with Noel as he was with me. We had no real songs as such. On that subject, Hendrix and I actually ended up in nose-to-nose confrontation on about the third rehearsal.

Jimi said, 'Well, we've got some gigs coming up, let's do . . . . "Midnight Hour".'

I, being a cocky little bastard at the time, said, 'Oh fuck! Not this *again*. I've just come from doing "Midnight Hour" for two years. We've got a new band, can't we do better than this? Please?' I had nothing against the song, great, a classic, but that was my attitude.

Because of this confrontation and the fact that I'd only agreed to the twenty quid for two weeks, I was branded by the management as 'The Troublemaker. This Boy is no good for us.' Words were had behind my back – not by Hendrix – after the second or third rehearsal, you know, 'Maybe he's not the right choice for us!' From what I understand they did actually try Aynsley Dunbar again, I'm not sure. Noel went with the flow, had to, long as he got his train fare,

but I think that, because I spoke my mind, Jimi rooted for me, he thought we would work well together.

Some of the rehearsals took place in the offices of a music publisher in Savile Row or Albemarle Street – a really straight music publisher. Jimi and Noel had these tiny little amps. Jimi said, 'Gotta get rid of this stuff!' He wanted big Marshall amplifiers. For a three-piece band we thought, let's make it powerful. The finance wasn't there at the time, but we were determined to get rid of those amps. We tried everything to break them: they got dropped down flights of stairs, we nearly threw them out of the windows. It took about three days, but in the end we managed it. I remember at one of the rehearsals Henry Mancini appeared at the door, with fingers in his ears. 'Hey, you guys, can't you keep it down a bit,' and this was with the small amps.

One thing that struck me about Jimi early on was his hands. He had these huge hands, his thumbs were nearly as long as his fingers. Like many blues players he could use it to his advantage hooking it over the neck of his guitar as an extra finger. But we're not talking 'secrets of his success' here because Jimi could, and did, play anything – left-handed, right-handed, upside down, behind his back and with his teeth. He probably could've played with his toe-nails.

The name of the band, 'The Jimi Hendrix Experience', was dreamed up by Chas, in the Gorham Hotel in New York just after meeting Jimi. The name, of course, was excellent because it could cover any number of members and types of material.

LEFT:
Jimi in dressing room.
Saville Theatre, London,
'67.

RIGHT:
Mitch with Georgie Fame
and The Blue Flames.
1965 London.

THE ONLY WORK THE NEW BAND HAD BEEN offered was as support on a short tour of France with French star Johnny Halliday. A curious start, but seemingly the only work Chas could get them at the time. It had arisen because Halliday had been in London and had spotted Jimi jamming with Brian Auger, probably at the Scotch of St James Club. It seems that Halliday had approached Chas and asked him whether Jimi could do the support. Chas replied that there'd be no problem – they'd be there in two weeks. Considering that auditions had barely started, things had to move pretty fast. It is tempting to speculate whether, if more time had been available, Chas and Jimi would have put something other than the three-piece together, something more along the lines of Chas's original concept. More academic, perhaps, is whether Halliday actually wanted a Hendrix band as a support. More likely he was over here scouting for musicians for *his* band, something he often did, and indeed, there were two English guys in the Halliday band, when The Experience joined them on tour.

Before the tour started Chas had been forced to sell a couple more of his basses, but it meant that Jimi and Noel got their coveted Marshall amps.

We had no road manager, just the three of us plus Chas. I remember getting on the plane in London and seeing these brand new Marshall cabinets being literally thrown into the hold. There were no flight cases, they were just wrapped in the original corrugated cardboard sheeting. We were thinking, 'Oh no, what are we going to find at the other end?' We hadn't got any spares and you're hardly going to pick up any of those bits and pieces in Paris or anywhere in France.

I don't remember the first gig per se, but we did 'Midnight Hour', 'Have Mercy', 'Land of a Thousand Dances', you know, the standards. We were only on for about fifteen minutes. Johnny Halliday was, and still is, sort of the Elvis Presley of France. You'd do these grubby little cinemas, right out in the sticks, much worse than the cinema tours you did back in England, real flea-pits. He was treated like royalty, however – given the keys to the city and all that. We also got treated really well. We had to muck in together – you find a lot out about each other under those conditions, very quickly.

Prior to that I hadn't known anything about Hendrix and where he came from, musically or otherwise. There'd been the casual reference to playing with Ike Turner, The Isley Brothers or whoever, not name-dropping, but those things gradually came out on the road. He was a quiet bloke – at least until he got on stage. It was on the first

Hey Joe/Stone Free Polydor 56 139 (12.66).

Jimi at work 1967

gig that we saw the whole other person, completely different from anything I'd seen before, even during rehearsals. I knew he played really tasty guitar, had the chops, but I didn't know about the showmanship that went with it. It was like – 'Whoosh! This man really is outfront!' I knew he wasn't that comfortable about singing – in fact he was really quite shy about it and Chas had to push him to some degree. He took a while to convince, but not really that long. The showmanship – playing it behind his head, with his teeth etc. – was amazing. But even

*First time in France
1966.*

huge horn section, were all French. On the first day on the road I got to sit next to this trombone player and my French is non-existent and his English wasn't much better. Anyway, I went through my suitcase, found this little piece of illegal smoking substance, sat down next to the trombone player again and attempted to roll a joint, which I did very badly.

The guy said, 'Oh Meesh, you like?' and I said, 'Well, you know, take it or leave it.'

After that, every night in the wings, I'd get this little nudge – 'Meesh, come with us.' And I'd go and have a smoke with the Halliday band. The atmosphere really loosened up and they really got to like Jimi and the rest of us. I'd worked in France before, but only TV things, so I had very little experience of French audiences. They don't clap! You'd finish off a number and . . . silence. You'd think, 'Christ, what's this?' 'Is it respect or do they hate us?' On the first few gigs they didn't know how to take us and didn't really want to see us. But it seems that we were going down quite well – we'd have been told pretty damn quickly if they really had hated us.

The main gig on the tour was the Paris Olympia, a big vaudeville theatre, not really a rock audience at all at that time. I think we did two nights, with a night off in between. We did our fifteen minutes each night, that was all we were allowed and we didn't know any more numbers anyway. We knew half a dozen numbers, maximum. We did actually go over time one night and got our wrists slapped.

I've been told that one of our sets was broadcast on Europe 1. It seems unlikely, but Halliday was massive, so his set might have been broadcast, and it's just possible ours was as well.

then it was obviously not just flashiness, he really did have the musicianship to go with it.

Those first gigs were strange though. We were on a tour bus, Halliday just turned up in his new Mustang or whatever. The rest of us were in this rickety old coach. There were two English guys in Halliday's band – Mick Jones, now with Foreigner and Tommy Brown who was the drummer from Nero And The Gladiators. They had worked together for some years, but they were the only other English guys, whereas the rest, including a

ON OCTOBER 23, SHORTLY AFTER RETURNING from France, the band booked into Kingsway Studios, in London, primarily to cut their first single. It was already agreed that this would be a version of 'Hey Joe', a number that Hendrix had regularly performed in New York, although Mitch is fairly sure that for some reason the band didn't work it out until their return from France. The story goes that Chas knew the song as well as Jimi and had decided that if he ever got to produce a band, he would get them to do 'Hey Joe' as he was sure it could be a hit. The story continues that as he walked into the Café Wha! that fateful day, Jimi was actually performing the song!

Apart from recording 'Hey Joe' the band also cut its B-side, the Hendrix original 'Stone Free'. What else, if anything, was done that day, has long been the subject of speculation. Legend has it that they recorded several numbers, including 'Land Of A Thousand Dances', 'Have Mercy' and 'Johnny B. Goode' as well as 'Hey Joe' and 'Stone Free'.

I'm sure we didn't record 'Thousand Dances' on any session. The others . . . well, I can't really see it. 'Hey Joe' was the thing we went for. Jimi knew the song – he'd done it in New York and Chas liked it. To the best of my memory we used the first version of 'Hey Joe'. I have a feeling that a little later we went into Regent Sound and may possibly have attempted it again on that session, but I'm sure that we used the original done at Kingsway. Once Hendrix had thought up and shown Noel that walking-bass part, at Kingsway, we'd got it down really quickly and any subsequent versions weren't as good.

I'm sure we did 'Wind Cries Mary' twice. That was at Kingsway again. We did a demo version on a Friday night and it was ragged, to put it mildly. We went off over the weekend, did some gigs, went back the following Tuesday and got it right, but the initial feeling wasn't there. So the original was released, warts and all. Thank goodness – it's one of my favourites.

I'm sure that not a lot of time was spent on 'Hey Joe'. Studio time was expensive and there simply wasn't the budget for endless recording. Also you have to remember that Chas had been in The Animals and that 'House of the Rising Sun' had cost like four quid or something to make. Rightly or wrongly he had the attitude that since that had got to No. 1 there was no need to piss

around in the studio wasting time and money.

'Stone Free' was a Hendrix original, of course. I don't know if he brought it over with him. After those initial words we'd had, you know 'Christ almighty, we must have some new material', he started writing really quickly. I think that he brought over a scrapbook with ideas and some of those got translated into proper songs, or at least sketches for songs that we worked out in the studio.

One thing I always found surprising about Jimi was that he'd not spent much time in the American school system. In fact they'd given him a rough time and by his own admission he didn't enjoy it, which is why he'd chosen to join the army at a young age. Despite that he was incredibly literate and in possession

BELOW:
Jimi relaxing during filming at the Saville Theatre, London, January '67.

of a great deal of wisdom. I've really no idea where it came from, but what a gift for words! Apart from anything else, it really came out when he started writing songs.

After Kingsway, I think we used Regent Sound once, but nothing from there was ever used. After that we moved into Olympic, which was a very bright move. The room was big enough and the equipment was good and they had excellent engineers. This was the 'second' Olympic in Barnes (south west London); they'd only just opened it and we always used the larger room.

RIGHT:
Ciggie break at Saville. London '67.

I always felt completely at home with Jimi, right from the beginning and him with me, right through to the end. The two of us working together – it was so easy. I know he always enjoyed my playing, as I did his. Listening back there were times, though, for whatever reasons – my inexperience, overenthusiasm, etc. – that I overplayed. There are several sessions that make me cringe, but you learn by experience. But it was always incredibly easy, I always knew where he was leading me and he was always prepared to be led by you. He was never frightened about going off in unknown directions, unlike a lot of otherwise very good players. You try and lead them off and you can feel them pull up, scared to try something new.

Often, what worked best in the studios was Jimi and I laying down the basic drum and guitar parts on our own and then later on adding the bass and other bits. In the early days, particularly, we recorded very quickly. 'Purple Haze', for example. Hendrix came in and kind of hummed us the riff and showed Noel the chords and the changes. I listened to it and we went, 'OK, let's do it.' We got it on the third take as I recall.

One problem with young, struggling bands that is usually overlooked – particularly when some of them aren't natives of the town they're working in – is how and where they live. This may sound like a mundane problem, but if you're broke and trying to commute into town for gigs and recordings, as Noel was, it was no minor matter.

When Noel first joined the band, he had nowhere to stay in London and used to try and get back to Folkestone. Quite soon he started complaining, and rightly so, about where he was supposed to live. For me it was OK, I could always stay with my folks in Ealing in west London, plus I had a car. Hendrix and Chas were in a hotel in Bayswater but Noel was still out on a limb.

Eventually he found a place with Gerry Stickells, our roadie, just one room, cold water and a curtain between the two beds. That wore a little bit thin after about a week

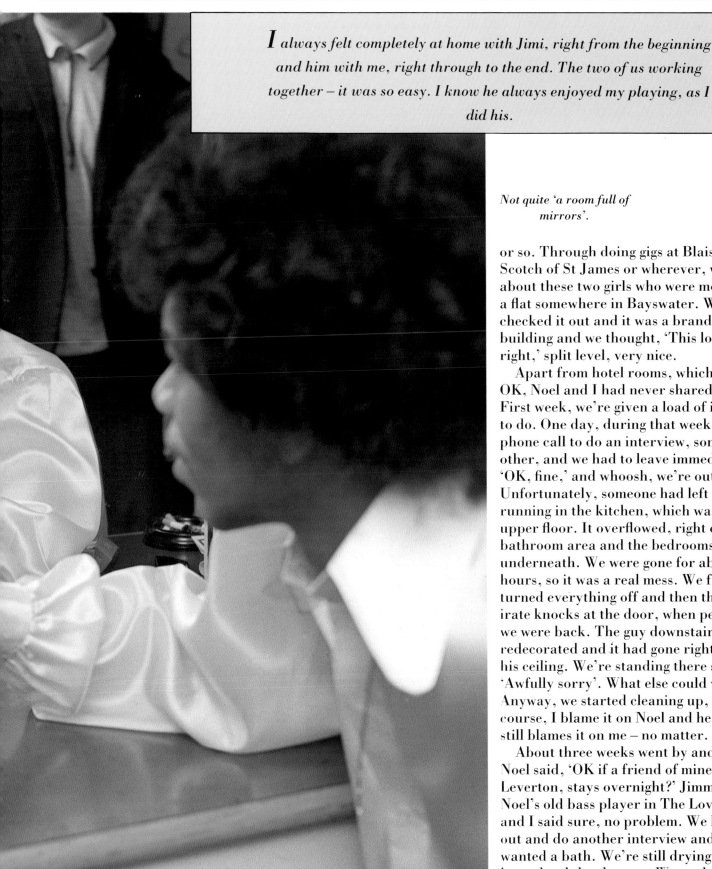

> *I always felt completely at home with Jimi, right from the beginning and him with me, right through to the end. The two of us working together – it was so easy. I know he always enjoyed my playing, as I did his.*

Not quite 'a room full of mirrors'.

or so. Through doing gigs at Blaises or the Scotch of St James or wherever, we did hear about these two girls who were moving out of a flat somewhere in Bayswater. We went and checked it out and it was a brand new building and we thought, 'This looks all right,' split level, very nice.

Apart from hotel rooms, which had been OK, Noel and I had never shared a place. First week, we're given a load of interviews to do. One day, during that week, we got a phone call to do an interview, somewhere or other, and we had to leave immediately. 'OK, fine,' and whoosh, we're out the door. Unfortunately, someone had left the water running in the kitchen, which was on the upper floor. It overflowed, right down to the bathroom area and the bedrooms which are underneath. We were gone for about four hours, so it was a real mess. We frantically turned everything off and then there were irate knocks at the door, when people knew we were back. The guy downstairs had just redecorated and it had gone right through his ceiling. We're standing there saying, 'Awfully sorry'. What else could we say? Anyway, we started cleaning up, and of course, I blame it on Noel and he probably still blames it on me – no matter.

About three weeks went by and one day Noel said, 'OK if a friend of mine, Jimmy Leverton, stays overnight?' Jimmy was Noel's old bass player in The Loving Kind, and I said sure, no problem. We had to go out and do another interview and Jimmy wanted a bath. We're still drying out the lower level, by the way. We got back and

Leverton is quaking at the door. Poor sucker, he's turned on the bath and the tap has literally exploded, come off in his hand. There's water hitting the ceiling and flooding everything. We left the flat that night. From there I moved around the corner to Graham Nash's place, whom I'd known for several years. He'd been sharing this mews house with one of The Walker Brothers, who happened to have just left.

Graham, of course, had had several years' experience of making hit records and dealing with management and after I moved in and got to know him better, he started giving me advice. He really used to piss Chas off, by asking questions like, 'Where's their publishing money going?' His experience had given rise to a certain scepticism about management. As it happens I played on a couple of Hollies' album tracks, when Bobby Elliot, their excellent drummer, contracted peritonitis and, of course, Graham came in and contributed background vocals on 'Axis Bold As Love'. Great voice! I enjoyed sharing with Graham – nice house, very pleasant. It was also a place where Hendrix could seek some refuge away from his flat in Upper Berkeley St. with Chas. No offence to Chas, but it was good for Hendrix to get away for an hour or so. Graham and Jimi would often play together at the house, and there was some thought given to them writing together, but I have the feeling that it was officially discouraged.

B Y COMMON AGREEMENT THE CLUB SCENE IN and around London in the mid-Sixties was the best in the world. It was certainly also the biggest, with hundreds of clubs dotted all over central London and the suburbs. This situation had been evolving since the early Fifties, resulting particularly from the growth of interest in jazz in post-war Britain. By the late Fifties jazz clubs were joined by folk clubs and for a brief time rock 'n' roll clubs as well.

The big explosion came in 1964, with the rapid success of The Rolling Stones and the arrival of British R&B. Allied to this was the sudden interest in fashion, particularly of course, Carnaby Street. Pop culture was every-

where. Despite the all-pervading pop 'image', not everyone looked the same or had the same tastes. There were mods, beatniks and left-over rockers; all with their own styles, music and clubs. Some of it was working-class, some – particularly the art-school/beatnik element – was more middle-class, and some aspects – despite the supposedly egalitarian ethics of the time – quite upper-class.

For the first couple of years things were reasonably homogeneous but when Hendrix arrived, in late 1966, they were starting to become somewhat fragmented. Partly this was occurring along the aforementioned class lines. R&B had more or less united the kids of the day, but by late 1966 most working-class kids (primarily the mods) were veering towards Soul and Motown; the art-school types, by contrast, favoured a more purist, if electric, blues style. The two groups, able to recognize each other by their increasingly obvious sartorial differences, treated one another with mutual contempt, although on the whole the one side (mods)

RIGHT:
Jimi. London '67.

BELOW:
Jimi & Noel. France 1966.

favoured 'tension' the other 'tolerance'.

Primarily these distinctions manifested themselves in the suburbs, where the majority of the kids lived, but the West End clubs, generally, catered for one group or the other. Thus at one end of Wardour Street was the Marquee, traditionally an art-school/blues hang out and at the other, the Flamingo, a tougher soul-music venue. Interestingly, the Flamingo was virtually the home base of Mitch's pre-Experience band, The Blue Flames.

Added to these two types of club there were a couple of others that should be mentioned. Firstly there were the essentially new 'Underground' establishments, like UFO, located in Tottenham Court Road. UFO was the centre for

the emerging avant-garde bands like Pink Floyd and Soft Machine and the audience, admittedly closely related to the older art-school types, were Britain's proto-hippies.

The final type of club to be mentioned were the ones that catered for the new 'aristocracy', the wombs of what the media considered to be the new classless society. In fact they were just the reverse. These were places where the youngbloods of the genuine 'aristocracy' allowed themselves to rub shoulders with the lower orders – providing they were interesting and had money. This basically amounted to pop stars, photographers, fashion designers and the odd East End gangster. These clubs, like Blaises, the Bag o' Nails, and the Scotch of St James, seemed far more glamorous and therefore news-worthy, than a sweaty basement full of otherwise ordinary kids.

Chas Chandler had good connections in a large section of the London pop world. While not exactly a 'star' in his own right, he had been in a successful band, The Animals, and consequent-ly knew all of the musicians and club-owners worth knowing in London. These contacts proved invaluable in launching Hendrix. First off he was able to introduce him to his musician friends and set up jamming situations for Jimi. More important was his ability to call in favours to get the new band gigs after the French tour. That really counted and even then, despite his friends, he found it very difficult. In terms of regular gigs all he was really able to manage, at the time, was a few gigs on the Ricky Tick club circuit and some one-offs at places like the Ram Jam in Brixton and the Upper Cut in East Ham. However, his major coup was to get the band what were essentially 'showcase' gigs at several of the up-market clubs like Blaises and the Scotch of St James. It was there that the press, other musicians and promoters saw the band in conducive surroundings. It was from those gigs that the word about the band began to spread, but those first couple of months were really tough.

After recording 'Hey Joe' we still had no gigs, as such, lined up. Somehow, though, we landed four nights at the Big Apple Club in Munich, in the second week of November. By this time Noel had grabbed hold of an old friend of his, Gerry Stickells, who was turned from a car mechanic into our road manager. He took the train out with the equipment and we went separately. We supported some kind of a soul review and actually went down very well. It was only a small place, full of GIs, but it was OK, a good gig.

After that we did what must have been our first real English gig (apart, I think, from a showcase thing at the Scotch of St James) at the Ricky Tick Club, in Hounslow, west London. The Ricky Tick circuit was run by Phil Hayward, who knew Chas from The Animals which is I guess how we got the gig.

I'd played there before with Georgie Fame and at the Windsor Ricky Tick. In comparison with the Windsor club, which was a real barn of a place, the Hounslow one was tiny, with a low ceiling. We were set up in a corner and had very little room to move. As I recall the audience weren't exactly hostile, but they didn't know what to make of us.

Most of our early gigs were like that. We were playing to audiences largely composed of mohair-suited mods and sort of proto-skinheads in boots and braces. They really didn't know how to take us – Jimi, especially – at all. We *were* well received at the showcases, like Blaises and the Bag o' Nails.

FAR LEFT:
Guitar strangler.
London '66.

LEFT:
About to embark on one
of our first trips abroad

The Experience performing live on British T.V. programme 'Ready, Steady, Go', December 1966. One of the group's earliest TV appearances.

The press liked us and so did other musicians, who turned up to hear Jimi play. That made a hell of lot of difference, it became a word of mouth thing, and spread very quickly. This was apart from any hype that went with it that Chas tried to promote.

Make no mistake, Chas did a great job in promoting what he obviously believed in. Within the first couple of gigs, he realized what sort of band and style Jimi wanted to be involved with. It was obviously something he himself hadn't initially considered – it was a long way from the matching suit, soul review thing he seems to have originally planned for Jimi. Once he'd seen what was in Jimi's mind, though, he did everything he could to bring Jimi out even further and to promote that.

The regular clubs we were playing were basically the old soul/R&B circuit that I and indeed Chas had come from and had connections with. That's the main reason

that Chas got us those gigs – they were the people he knew and probably they were the *only* gigs he could get.

The thing with the UFO and Middle Earth type of Underground clubs was that, for whatever reason, they didn't want to know us at that time anyway. Looking back we might seem to have had more in common with that audience, but maybe Chas thought they were rather marginal and wanted to build some kind of base for us. He was basically sticking with what he knew and although at those initial gigs they didn't know what to make of us, in the long term it was probably a smart move.

It did take a while to get regular gigs – we didn't even have one on New Year's Eve '66, so Noel said, 'Come down to Folkestone, I know this little club.' We went down by train and it was *freezing*. The club was Tofts, also known as Stan's and it was like a youth club – it made the Ricky Tick look like a palace.

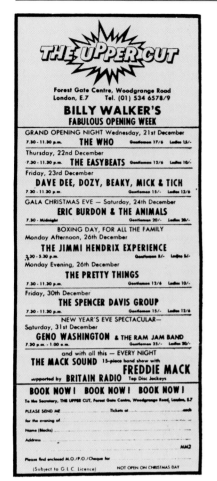

LEFT:
*Some early posters. We
were down the billing in
those days – they
couldn't even get our
name right!*

LEFT:
*Jack, Phyl and Mitch
Mitchell, Ealing, London
1980.*

It was OK, no one knew how to take us, but they accepted us since they knew Noel as it was his local club.

Anyway Noel's mum, Margaret, who Jimi and I both loved, said, 'Come back to our place afterwards.' So we packed into two minicabs and drove for what seemed like forever. As we crowded in, shivering, Jimi said to Margaret 'Let me stand next to your fire'. Margaret believes and I would back her, that that's where the idea for the song came from. It was a little bungalow on the coast and a good night was had by all. We all kipped down under blankets and overcoats. Jimi though, and his girlfriend Cathy Etchingham, got one of the beds. It was one of those fun things that made the band more cohesive.

Jimi never complained and was probably amazed at some of the English hospitality he experienced. Most people took to him very well; he was always a complete gentleman.

He loved my folks, the house where they lived was not far from Heathrow Airport and if we ever missed a flight we'd drive over there. Jimi loved to sit and have a drink with my mum and dad.

In mid-January '67 we had a brief residency at the 7½ Club in White Horse Street in Mayfair. The place had been in existence for several years under various names and was another up-market Blaises kind of place, only smaller. That was where Mick Jagger, McCartney and all those people came to see us. Brigitte Bardot came down one night as well. It was another showcase for us, we played there about five times in a week. In fact I think it was our last showcase gig. We'd already started playing the provinces by then.

Strangely enough our early out-of-town gigs, especially the northern ones, were really easy: the crowds were really receptive from the word go.

'BOUT THE CIRCUS
and
THE WISHING WELL

BY THE END OF JANUARY 1967, THE Experience had acquired a degree of fame in Britain and a fair amount of notoriety. 'Hey Joe' was a hit, if not a huge one (it reached No. 6 and its follow-up, 'Purple Haze' made No. 3) and the band had appeared on the two leading British pop TV programmes, *Ready Steady Go!* and *Top of the Pops.* Press on the whole had been kind, picking up on Hendrix's undoubted talents as a guitarist and the sheer power and orginality of the band. At the same time, thanks largely to the talents of Chas and a few sympathetic journalists like Keith Altham, Hendrix was being portrayed as some kind of demonic, wild beast. Although his performances might have led the public (those that had seen him, at least) to believe that this was how Hendrix really behaved, it was, of course, a long way from the real truth. It didn't matter – there was no such thing as bad publicity and the public lapped it up.

In reality, although attracting national publicity the band had hardly played outside London, apart from their jaunts to France and Germany and a trip to the States was still some off. The early months of 1967 saw them attempting to rectify this situation, at least with regard to Europe and the rest of the UK.

For The Experience their warm welcome in northern England was a pleasant surprise, because, with the band's radical music and appearance, northerners, with their reputation for being conservative in such matters, might have been expected to take exception to them. Bands like Pink Floyd suffered greatly outside of London, frequently meeting a barrage of incomprehension and bottles. In fact the only violence The Experience encountered came from the police.

One of the first gigs up north was at the New Century Hall in Manchester on a Saturday night (January 7). We went back to our hotel after we'd played, changed our clothes and decided to go to the clubs to see what was going on – places like the Twisted Wheel. I knew the club owners well from Blue Flames days, but none of them would let us in. 'Sorry Mitch, can't let you in, come back in an hour's time.'

It turned out the police were busting people for being under-age or something. After about the third club we walked over to the car and suddenly Noel and I were grabbed and slung against the railings of the police station. We got slapped around a few times and I was going, 'What the fuck's going on?'

They were the police, but we didn't believe it at first, they were all in plain clothes. They took Hendrix's passport off him, but left him alone as he was an American, but they hung

Purple Haze/
51st Anniversary
Track 604 001 (3.67)

RIGHT AND BELOW:
Jimi and Mitch at
London's Marquee Club,
January 1967.

Noel on the railings. They searched the car but didn't find anything. It really shook us up though. We went back to the hotel, phoned up Mike Jeffery and managed to get through for once. Eventually two cops were thrown off the force because of it. It only got reported in one paper though, the *Sheffield Sunday Examiner* or whatever.

That aside though, it was really good up north. Again we played the same circuit as I'd done with The Blue Flames, the Mojo in Sheffield, the Twisted Wheel, clubs in Darlington and South Shields and a bit later the Club a Go-Go in Newcastle. That, of course, had been The Animals' home base early on and was still owned by Mike Jeffery.

As a band, we rarely, if ever, experienced any violence. In my early days in bands, however, I remember going up to Barrowlands Ballroom, in Glasgow, where if they threw bottles at you, they liked you. They had chicken wire in front of the stage there, like that scene in *The Blues Brothers*.

Hendrix had been through all that too, on the 'chitlin' circuit' – those were the common experiences that all bands had. If you were

ABOVE:
Jimi struttin' the stuff, Germany, March 1967.

in a band you were in a band, you knew about all that stuff and accepted it together – colour never entered into it at all, certainly not in England. English audiences were used to integrated bands and maybe that was a difference for Hendrix, experiencing that possibly for the first time outside Greenwich Village.

Noel and I never really understood the pressures an American black person went through, until later on at the start of the Monkees' tour in Jacksonville, somewhere in the Deep South anyway. Hendrix wouldn't go into certain restaurants or stores with us, we'd say, 'Hey, why not?' and he'd go, 'No I do not want to go in there.'

Some of it he could treat as a joke. Later on the Monkees' tour for instance, where Screen Gems and Columbia were paying for everything in sight, we had a limo driver who was definitely Ku Klux Klan, and Hendrix made a point of sitting in the front passenger seat. He was *his* driver for the afternoon. Noel and I thought it was funny at the time, which it was in itself, but thinking about it later, we suddenly realized what was really

> *In my early days in bands, however, I remember going up to Barrowlands Ballroom, in Glasgow where if they threw bottles at you, they liked you. They had chicken wire in front of the stage there, like that scene in The Blues Brothers.*

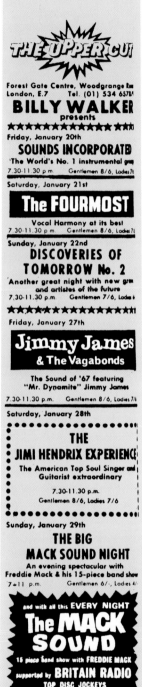

LEFT:
The Jimi Hendrix Experience on tour in England, early 1967.

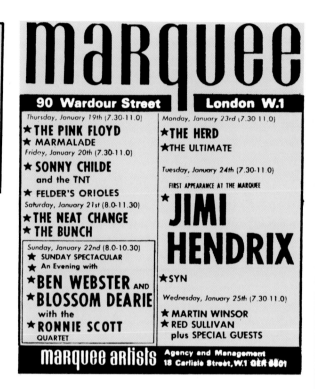

going on.

The potential racial problems were also magnified by people disliking not just Jimi for being black *per se*, but because he was playing with two white boys. So we became aware of racial tensions pretty quickly – I have to say that there was never any problem *ever* within the band.

In the later stages of his life there was pressure put on him from various sources to work with black musicians and to become more of a spokesman for black people. I think he gave it consideration and tried to do that, but he found out that it didn't really work. It was a conflict within himself that he never really resolved. The bottom line, I think, for him was, 'I'm an artist, I don't care what your colour is, if we work together well, that's all that matters.' He was the first person to say, 'Fuck you' if people got on his back too much about working for 'the cause'.

The band was never allowed to play at the Apollo Theater in Harlem, which was a great annoyance to Jimi. Basically, the management didn't want us and supposedly we didn't have a black audience at that time.

Actually it turned out later that we did have a black audience, even quite early on. We only discovered this later, after Jimi's death sadly, so he never really knew.

The thing with the Apollo was odd, though. We knew, for example, that The Animals had done it – one of the few white acts to play the venue. I went up there on one of my first visits to America and had real trouble getting a cab to take me. It might've been the way we looked, of course. We also had trouble finding hotels to take us in New York – we got asked to leave about five in one day. We'd booked in and they'd take one look at us and claim they were full up – just bloody amazing. Mind you, visually, we stood out a mile from our audiences, particularly early on.

Jimi, from things I'd gathered, had always

The Wind Cries Mary/
Highway Chile Track 604
004 (5.67)

OPPOSITE:

*Jimi, Mitch and Noel
during the photo session
which produced the 'Are
You Experienced' album
cover.*
BELOW:
US sleeve of first album.

ARE YOU EXPERIENCED U.K. Track 613 001 (5.67) US Reprise RS 6261

SIDE 1   Foxy Lady; Manic Depression; Red House; Can You See Me; Love Or Confusion; I Don't
         Live Today.
SIDE 2   May This Be Love; Fire; Third Stone From The Sun; Remember; Are You Experienced.

All Titles written by Jimi Hendrix. Produced by Chas Chandler. Engineered by Eddie Kramer.
(Note: The U.S. version of the album drops 'Red House'; 'Can You See Me' & 'Remember' and
replaces them with the first three single a sides).

worn flamboyant clothes, even as a kid. He
told me he'd been suspended from junior
high-school once for wearing bright red
trousers! Before he came over to London, I
believe that most of his wardrobe had been
seized by the management of the hotel he was
living in in New York because he couldn't pay
the bill. He basically arrived here with one
pair of trousers and one pair of shoes. The
Burberry raincoat, was, I suspect what he
thought he *ought* to wear in England.

Gradually he did acquire a new wardrobe,
like the old army jacket from Portobello
Road, which was as much cheap and
cheerful as anything deliberately hip.

Jimi was being subsidized by Chas to some
degree and rightly so, but Noel and I
couldn't afford new clothes. Shops like
Granny Takes a Trip, in the King's Road,
used to make things up for Jimi, which may
have led to a little resentment, but he was the
front man, so it was justified. Things did
come to a head at one point and Chas did
buy Noel and I one stage outfit apiece, which
for a perspiring drummer was not the most
comfortable of articles.

In time, of course, I got my hair permed.
Noel didn't have to bother, his was natural.
For him it was a case of 'I get up in the
morning and run me hands through me hair

Jimi with The Who (l to r) Roger Daltrey, Pete Townshend, Jimi, John Entwhistle, Keith Moon, London, January 1967.

and the sparrows fly out.' Hendrix was into Carmen hair rollers at that point, among other bits and pieces. Anyway, I used to come off stage wringing wet, couldn't do a thing with my hair which would be completely limp and I thought, 'Blow this, everyone else round here seems to have an easy time, I'll go and get it permed, at least you don't have to muck around.' So I went to see this young lady who worked for a hairdresser and was supposed to know what she was doing and had the perm.

Apparently what they should do is to cut your hair first before they perm it. She didn't and it ended up sticking out about a mile, it was like Art Garfunkel . . . expanded. Generally, though, it was much easier to deal with, and I guess it gave us an overall image, which was good for the mags and music media at that time.

FEBRUARY AND MARCH OF 1967 SAW THE BAND criss-crossing Britain in the time-honoured fashion of the emerging British rock band, playing at such wonderful locations as the Cellar Club, South Shields, the Blue Moon, Cheltenham and the Sinking Ship, Stockport, not to mention London dates at both the Marquee and the Flamingo, plus the more prestigious Saville Theatre (where they ultimately played three times). The band enjoyed most of them, but the last gig of the tour was soured by the tragic death of Brian Epstein who owned the Saville Theatre. The band were forced to cancel the second show which they felt was the last thing Brian would have wanted.

By and large most of this tour has slipped from the memory. Mitch does recall, however, the famous Gliderdrome in Boston, Lincolnshire. This was Jimi's first (and presumably last) encounter with a legendary eccentric local who conducted the band from in front of the stage, complete with baton and full evening dress. The Experience were not the first band he'd conducted, he'd been doing it since the Forties and over a cup of tea in the dressing room, would tell the visiting band all of the famous names he'd conducted in the past. The Gliderdrome also had revolving stages which passed through an archway, unfortunately not as high as equipment stacked on the stage. As The Experience majestically whirled off, all their amps came toppling down over them.

By early 1967 the band were regularly sandwiching record sessions for their first album between dates on their ever-bulging gig itinerary. In fact a few tracks including, probably, 'Third Stone From The Sun' were laid down, at least in basic form, at the end of 1966 at the Olympic studios in Kingsway, London. 'Third Stone From The Sun' was easily the most ambitious track on the 'Are You Experienced' album but the creation of such masterworks was not the primary concern of the album.

Despite the presence of a fair amount of experimentation in the studio, 'Are You Experienced' was the live Experience on record. Most of the songs we did live, some only occasionally like 'Manic Depression' and 'Third Stone From The Sun', but as a whole it became the basis of the live act for some time to come. There were a few we didn't do live, such as 'Remember' and 'May This Be Love', because in all honesty they were album fillers, not because we couldn't re-create them on stage.

We really were a 'band' at that time. Hendrix would have an idea of chords and structure; he wrote 'songs'. When it came to rhythmic structure, everything was left up to me and Noel. Noel has complained over the years that he didn't want to be told what to play, but things were actually more flexible than that. Jimi would say to him, 'This is the way the song goes, these are the notes that are available, but around that structure you can play anything you want.'

There isn't much left over from the first two albums, in terms of out-takes or different versions, purely because of the way

Laundry day for Noel. Jimi's flat, May 1967.

*Left:
Will the phone never ring? Jimi at home, London, May 1967.*

Playing Risk at Chas and Jimi's flat. London, May 1967.

I didn't realize for a while how many English players Jimi had heard, including, at the time, less well-known ones like Peter Green. Green in fact gave Hendrix a great run for his money and was one of the few guitarists who wasn't in awe of him, you know, he didn't say, 'Oh God, I've seen Hendrix, I'm gonna die!'

ABOVE:
Enjoying the marquee,
March 1967.

ABOVE LEFT:
Jimi's got The Blues,
January 1967.

ABOVE RIGHT:
Afternoon session in the
Marquee Club for
German TV, early 1967.

we worked. There was an incredible pressure on us – the cost of studio time and the fact that by early 1967 we were touring so much – but there are some things. There are a few songs that I, and apparently Noel as well, had completely forgotten about. Completely surprised me. I only heard them once a couple of years ago; they sounded rough – warts and all – but I enjoyed them. Hopefully they'll see the light of day. The ones I heard were Hendrix originals, but I know it's rumoured that we did a studio version of 'Like A Rolling Stone'. Now I don't remember it, but it makes sense that we should have recorded it early on. The fact that I'd forgotten these other songs means that things like 'Rolling Stone' might exist, but I just don't know. Hendrix was certainly a huge Dylan fan and he turned me on to Dylan.

Olympic was also a great place to experiment. One of the things that attracted Hendrix to working in England was that he'd heard the sounds that people like Jeff Beck – whose playing we all loved – were producing with fuzzboxes and wanted to work in English studios. Jeff was already known, quite rightly, as one helluva player. In fact I didn't realize for a while how many English players Jimi had heard, including, at the time, less well-known ones like Peter Green.

Green in fact gave Hendrix a great run for his money and was one of the few guitarists who wasn't in awe of him, you know, he didn't say, 'Oh God, I've seen Hendrix, I'm gonna die!'

Jimi was always so receptive and he really learned a lot from English players. He also taught me a lot. In the early days he turned me on to a lot of blues, like Robert Johnson. My blues background had been much more jazz-oriented, people like King Pleasure and Mose Allison. I knew about Muddy Waters and those people, but it took Hendrix to turn me on to other stuff. If it had been an English blues purist, like John Mayall, telling me all this, I doubt if I'd have listened, but being as it was Hendrix and he'd been through all of that, I did. Also he always did it in a very delicate way, just pointing out certain reference points.

And it was reciprocal: I'd say, well, try this – and I'd play him some Roland Kirk or Miles Davis or even a bit of Coltrane. It wasn't that we were picking each others' brains, it wasn't a self-conscious kind of process. With Noel it was usually 'Ere, have you heard the new Small Faces record?' For all the years we were on the road Noel had a Small Faces album and a Byrds album and a portable record player. We always knew which hotel room *he* was in!

LEFT:
T.V. show in Amsterdam, March 1967.

RIGHT:
Mitch at The Olympia, Paris, September 1967.

BELOW:
Paris May 1967.

A S EARLY AS THE BEGINNING OF MARCH 1967, it became apparent to all concerned that the band were taking off in Europe, or more exactly, France, Holland, Germany and Scandinavia, and from this point on they spent as much time there as anywhere else, except ultimately, the States.

We did become very big in Europe very quickly. The word seemed to spread in a very short space of time, which was surprising for all of us. Aside from the Johnny Halliday tour, Jimi hadn't worked in Europe at all. Noel had to a limited degree, he'd played in the German clubs as a teenager, as every British band did, but it was his first real exposure to a larger crowd. I'd done quite a few of the Swedish and German gigs before with The Blue Flames, so I knew most of the venues.

The Germans in particular seemed very

receptive. We did the inevitable Star Club in Hamburg early on (March 17–19) but not the six-shows-a-day routine. We just did a Friday, Saturday and Sunday-night stint, we didn't have to do the whole matinée thing – the Star Club was winding down a bit by then anyway. There was an Israeli band on who were doing the full six-weeks, five-shows-a-day deal. They were a sort of Beach Boys, harmony cover band. Anyway it was their last night while we were there and during their final break we retuned their guitars up an octave. Obviously they just rushed back, grabbed their guitars, bang, on stage. It was as though someone had tightened their jock-straps.

Most places in Europe that we hit, we did broadcasts, even if it meant getting up at the crack of dawn and going out and miming to your latest record in a field, while it was snowing. We used to think, 'What the hell are we doing this for?', but obviously it paid off in terms of publicity. The thing that always amazed me with the German fans was how much information they had about us. They knew stuff about Jimi from years back, not just the standard press-release info.

Most of the places we played in Europe were small theatres, there were no real blues-clubs, I don't think they existed as they did in England. We did do a couple of really weird gigs on the outskirts of Paris, though. They were almost like biker bars, really awful places. I don't know about those, but a lot of our early European gigs came from promoters seeing us at the early London showcase gigs.

We also did a graduation ball in Paris in March 1967, a really plush place. There was an oompah band on before us and they would not leave the stage. I remember one of our roadies, in a final act of desperation pushing the trombonist's slide back into his mouth – blood and teeth everywhere. We finally set up and played a few numbers and for some reason this huge fight broke out. They were fighting everywhere, up and down the stairs – all over the place. It got completely out of hand, so we left the gear and got the hell out.

IN BETWEEN TRIPS TO EUROPE, THE GROUP were placed on their first curious tour or bill (if you discount the Halliday tour) but as it turned out, not their last. This time it was a standard British Pop Package Tour. Since the late Fifties these tours had been the standard method of taking pop to the masses. The idea was simple: you took, say, five popular groups or singers plus a couple of unknown opening acts, bus them round the country in an old coach, stopping off for a series of shows in provincial towns and bracket them at either end by 'prestige' gigs in London. Almost without exception the venues were large, old cinemas. The two top acts got about half an hour each, the lower acts about 15–20 minutes and the opening acts were lucky to get ten. Everybody did the package tours, The Beatles and Stones included, and they were, if nothing else, the next step up from the clubs and ballrooms. The difference, though, was the audience, whose average age was about thirteen and whose primary intention – the girls, at least – was to scream their way through their favourite act. It was not, to say the least, an appropriate audience for The Experience and the only thing they had in common with the other acts was that they'd had a couple of hit singles – after that all resemblance ended.

BELOW:
Spot the Round Peg in The Square Hole – Jimi, Walker Brothers Tour April 1967. (l to r, Jimi, Cat Stevens, Gary Leeds, Engelbert Humperdinck at The Adelphi, Slough, England.

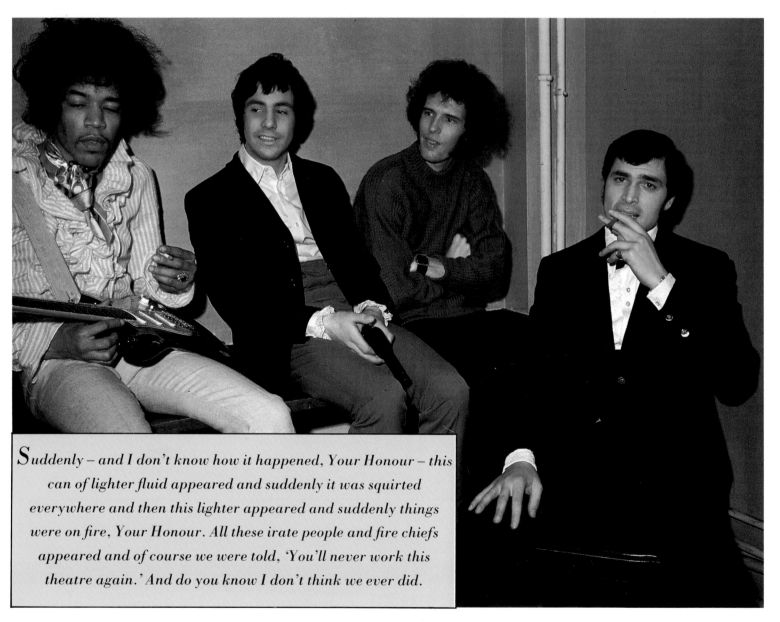

Suddenly – and I don't know how it happened, Your Honour – this can of lighter fluid appeared and suddenly it was squirted everywhere and then this lighter appeared and suddenly things were on fire, Your Honour. All these irate people and fire chiefs appeared and of course we were told, 'You'll never work this theatre again.' And do you know I don't think we ever did.

Taking care of business, Jimi, April 1967.

Yeah, the infamous Walker Brothers tour – The Walkers, Engelbert Humperdinck, Cat Stevens and a couple of opening acts. It was definitely not our kind of audience – but, then, what audience did we have at that time?

The first few gigs really didn't go well. Once again they didn't know what to make of us and we hadn't adjusted to the whole package tour thing. The major event of the tour was the Finsbury Park Astoria in London, where Hendrix set fire to his guitar for the first time.

To tell you the truth, I didn't know much about it. I saw Jimi mucking around in the dressing room with lighter fluid and there's lots of giggling going on. Anyway we went on and Hendrix has done the act, playing with

his teeth and all that. Suddenly – and I don't know how it happened, Your Honour – this can of lighter fluid appeared and suddenly it was squirted everywhere and then this lighter appeared and suddenly things were on fire, Your Honour. All these irate people and fire chiefs appeared and of course we were told, 'You'll never work this theatre again.' And do you know I don't think we ever did. Because of the Monterey film the burning guitar became part of the legend, but in fact he hardly ever did it, it happened maybe two or three times.

There wasn't too much interaction between the bands. Cat Stevens wouldn't travel on the coach after the first two days, because he thought we, The Experience,

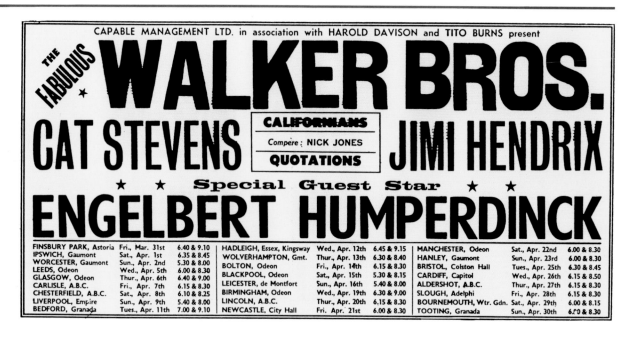

CAPABLE MANAGEMENT LTD. in association with HAROLD DAVISON and TITO BURNS present

THE FABULOUS **WALKER BROS.**

CAT STEVENS

CALIFORNIANS
Compere: NICK JONES
QUOTATIONS

JIMI HENDRIX

★ ★ Special Guest Star ★ ★

ENGELBERT HUMPERDINCK

FINSBURY PARK, Astoria	Fri., Mar. 31st	6.40 & 9.10	HADLEIGH, Essex, Kingsway	Wed., Apr. 12th	6.45 & 9.15	MANCHESTER, Odeon	Sat., Apr. 22nd	6.00 & 8.30
IPSWICH, Gaumont	Sat., Apr. 1st	6.35 & 8.45	WOLVERHAMPTON, Gmt.	Thur., Apr. 13th	6.30 & 8.40	HANLEY, Gaumont	Sun., Apr. 23rd	6.00 & 8.30
WORCESTER, Gaumont	Sun., Apr. 2nd	5.30 & 8.00	BOLTON, Odeon	Fri., Apr. 14th	6.15 & 8.30	BRISTOL, Colston Hall	Tues., Apr. 25th	6.30 & 8.45
LEEDS, Odeon	Wed., Apr. 5th	6.00 & 8.30	BLACKPOOL, Odeon	Sat., Apr. 15th	5.30 & 8.15	CARDIFF, Capitol	Wed., Apr. 26th	6.15 & 8.50
GLASGOW, Odeon	Thur., Apr. 6th	6.40 & 9.00	LEICESTER, de Montfort	Sun., Apr. 16th	5.40 & 8.00	ALDERSHOT, A.B.C.	Thur., Apr. 27th	6.15 & 8.30
CARLISLE, A.B.C.	Fri., Apr. 7th	6.15 & 8.30	BIRMINGHAM, Odeon	Wed., Apr. 19th	6.30 & 9.00	SLOUGH, Adelphi	Fri., Apr. 28th	6.15 & 8.30
CHESTERFIELD, A.B.C.	Sat., Apr. 8th	6.10 & 8.25	LINCOLN, A.B.C.	Thur., Apr. 20th	6.15 & 8.30	BOURNEMOUTH, Wtr. Gdn.	Sat., Apr. 29th	6.00 & 8.15
LIVERPOOL, Empire	Sun., Apr. 9th	5.40 & 8.00	NEWCASTLE, City Hall	Fri. Apr. 21st	6.00 & 8.30	TOOTING, Granada	Sun., Apr. 30th	6.00 & 8.30
BEDFORD, Granada	Tues., Apr. 11th	7.00 & 9.10						

were loonies. God knows why. He eventually came back because he thought he was missing out but we could have done without the companionship. On the matinée of the last show, when he was doing his hit, 'I'm Gonna Get Me A Gun', I placed this mechanical robot, which I'd bought, on stage. Its chest opened up and all these little machine guns started blazing away. He tried to kick it off stage, but this thing refused to die. He didn't take the joke too well. Anyway I retrieved it and put it on stage for The Walkers, when Scott was singing, 'My Ship Is Coming In'. He took it a lot better.

IF NOTHING ELSE THE WALKER BROTHERS TOUR was a shining example of a simple truth – the onstage sound in those days was invariably bad and equipment was at best unreliable. What you could get away with in the confines of a small club could become a disaster in a large hall. Today, even the lowliest bands expect a decent PA and onstage monitors, so that they can all hear each other and, although equipment failure isn't unknown, it's become a rarity. Those were different times.

In those days our equipment was always packing up. Early on we started using Marshall amps and in general their gear was more reliable, but you were dealing with a lot more power; Jim Marshall was trying to build 200 watt amplifiers and we were the guinea pigs.

I remember the first gig we ever did with those and immediately, within the first ten seconds, whoosh, everything had gone. Drummers, of course, weren't miked up at all, there was no PA as such, just whatever came with the venue, no back line, no monitors. I could barely hear anything at all, you really had to rely on watching people's hands move and hope you were playing in the same time; very difficult. You couldn't hear any vocals and half the time neither could the audience. We did get vocal monitors for front stage, but nothing for the fold back, certainly nothing for me.

Later on when we were headlining in the States I thought, 'Sod this', and bought four huge Voice of the Theatre speakers to use as makeshift monitors, but it was far from perfect. Not being able to hear meant that I had no real idea of how the band sounded live.

When we played Winterland in San Francisco in October '68, we were on the same bill as Buddy Miles' Express and I asked Buddy if he would take over for a couple of numbers, so that I could go out into the audience and listen to the band. It was a revelation. I wish the technology had been available then; it would have changed things to a giant degree.

MONTEREY
and too much
MONKEE BUSINESS

WITH BRITAIN AND A SUBSTANTIAL PART OF Europe convinced of their talents, a situation achieved in less than six months, The Experience began to consider the possibilities of doing the same in the States. However, with no US record deal signed and only a small word-of-mouth following, simply getting there was going to be difficult.

'Hey Joe' was finally released in the US in May; it failed to chart but a fateful phone call was then received from John Phillips of The Mamas & The Papas. Would The Experience play at a festival he was helping to organize, to be held in Monterey, the following month? They wouldn't be paid (none of the acts would) but all expenses would be covered. The answer was yes, provided they could take Brian Jones along to introduce the band.

The initial concept – the brainchild of LA Concert promoter Alan Pariser – was of a cross between the San Remo Song Festival (with its emphasis on unknown acts) and the Newport Jazz Festival. Pariser took the idea to Ben Shapiro, an LA showbiz promoter of many years' standing, who liked the idea, but not its proposed non-profit-making concept. They decided on Monterey, partly because it was already the site of an established annual jazz festival and partly because, given the assumption that it was to be somewhere in California, it should be midway between Los Angeles and San Francisco.

MUSIC · LOVE · FLOWERS

THE FOLLOWING ARTISTS WILL PERFORM

FRIDAY NIGHT JUNE 16 · 9·00 PM
ERIC BURDON AND THE ANIMALS   LOU RAWLS
THE ASSOCIATION   JOHNNY RIVERS
BEVERLY   SIMON AND GARFUNKEL
THE PAUPERS

SATURDAY AFTERNOON JUNE 17 · 1·30 PM
BIG BROTHER AND THE HOLDING COMPANY   THE ELECTRIC FLAG
PAUL BUTTERFIELD BLUES BAND   HUGH MASEKELA
CANNED HEAT   STEVE MILLER BLUES BAND
COUNTRY JOE AND THE FISH   QUICKSILVER MESSENGER SERVICE

SATURDAY EVENING JUNE 17 · 8·15 PM
THE BEACH BOYS   HUGH MASEKELA
BOOKER T AND THE MG'S   MOBY GRAPE
THE BYRDS   LAURA NYRO
JEFFERSON AIRPLANE   OTIS REDDING

SUNDAY AFTERNOON JUNE 18 · 1·30 PM
RAVI SHANKAR

SUNDAY EVENING JUNE 18 · 8·00 PM
THE BLUES PROJECT   THE MAMAS AND THE PAPAS
THE BUFFALO SPRINGFIELD   SCOTT McKENZIE
GRATEFUL DEAD   DIONNE WARWICK
THE JIMI HENDRIX EXPERIENCE   THE WHO

ALL STAR HOUSEBAND
DRUMS –	HAL BLAINE	HORNS	
PIANO –	LARRY KNECTEL	OLLIE MITCHEL	JIM HORN
BASS –	JOE OSBORN	FRED HILL	TEDDY EDWARDS
GUITAR –	AL DASY	LOU McCREARY	
VIBES –	GARY COLMAN	LOU BLACKBURN	

THEY MADE THE WORLD RING & SING WITH MUSIC & ELOQUENCE!

LEFT:
'Menu' *from Monterey*
U.S.A., *June 1967.*

RIGHT:
Jimi live *in Europe, May*
1967.

BELOW:
Brian Jones, Olympic
Studios, London 1967.

ABOVE:
Jimi Hendrix
Experience, first
American performance!
Monterey Pop Festival
U.S.A. June 1967.

RIGHT:
Jimi, back in the U.S.A.
Monterey, June 1967.

The lease for the site was signed on April 11 and the two promoters set about signing up the acts. They approached The Mamas & The Papas who accepted and John Phillips also agreed to help organize the affair, but only if they returned to the non-profit idea. Seeing the writing on the wall, Shapiro backed off, allowing himself to be bought out; the festival was left in the hands of Phillips and his manager Lou Adler as directors, with Pariser staying on as producer.

Given the minimal time they had (although the lease had been signed, the town didn't give its blessing until mid May) the organizers did a remarkable job. In musical terms a few acts they would have specifically liked did escape the net

– these included The Beatles (not a practical possibility), The Stones (two of whom were involved in legal battles), Cream, The Lovin' Spoonful and The Beach Boys (who originally agreed but backed out at the last minute). They also largely failed in their stated aim of providing a genuine cross-section of current pop music (Otis Redding was, with the exception of Hendrix and Lou Rawls, the only American black artist to appear) and with few exceptions they came up with a diet of new-style white rock. Indeed fourteen of the acts played what may loosely be described as Californian acid-rock and for better or worse the festival (and the resulting film) provided the commercial launching pad for many of those acts and the surrounding culture. This was certainly true for Big Brother And The Holding Company (with Janis Joplin), The Who and, perhaps more than any, Jimi Hendrix.

We'd been looking forward to going to the States, for the first time in my life and Noel's. There we were, first-class seats on TWA, Eric Burdon was on the flight and so was Brian Jones. We landed in New York and we're whisked off to the hotel in the limos. Noel and I were sharing a room and first off Noel decides to have a bath.

I'm unpacking the case and I hear this screech and Noel's standing on the side of the bath and I'm going, 'What's wrong, what's wrong?'. It was our first experience of cockroaches. There were loads of them. Mr Calm here says, 'Don't panic, I'll go into the kitchenette to find some powder or something.' So I open the drawer in the kitchen cabinet and it's the wrong move. The rest of the family are in there, thousands of them. Quick phone call to Chas, 'Get us out of here *now*.' We managed to transfer to another hotel, which was OK.

I remember that first night we met Deering Howe, an old friend of Chas's whose grandfather made the combine harvesters. He had this yacht and we were treated very regally. It was an amazing situation, first night in New York and we're sailing round the Hudson and the East River in this yacht – very decadent.

After that we flew to San Francisco, stayed a few hours there and then the next morning we flew on to Monterey. We had a private plane hired by the festival organizers and among the other passengers was Tiny Tim. We'd certainly never seen anybody like him before, warbling away with his ukelele.

After we checked in at the hotel I went out and looked over the site and I was amazed at the preparation that had gone into it all. I'd had no idea of how big an event it was going to be. I was walking around and it was quiet, just people setting up equipment.

I had some strawberries and as I was

The Experience backstage. France, May 1967.

eating them this guy comes up to me and says, 'Hey, they look nice, can I have one?'

I replied, 'Sure, here you are.'

He said, 'That's very kind of you – open your hand. In fact put both your hands out. In fact put the strawberries down.'

I'm not sure what's going on, but I put them down and he puts this gigantic quantity of these purple pills into my hands. Of course it's Owsley, the legendary acid chemist. I had heard of him, and knew of his reputation, but I wasn't sure what to do with these things, so I just stuffed them in my pocket, said, 'Thank you', and walked off.

That evening and the next day we saw a few of the acts. Otis Redding with most of Booker T And The MG's was amazing. Some of it wasn't so good, but after Otis maybe we were expecting too much. Other bands like The Byrds, great records, one of our favourite bands, but we thought they were having a bad night. Some bands, like The Jefferson Airplane, we'd heard of, but this was our first exposure to them. We were aware of the West Coast movement, but hadn't paid much attention to it until then. Some of them turned out to be very good, but we still thought, 'Well, if this is the best they can do . . . can't wait to play. Let me up on stage, we'll show these mothers.' I was amazed at the crowd and dare I say it the 'vibes', man!

We played on the Sunday night and, of course, it got down to who was going to follow whom, or Who as the case may be. The story of Townshend and Hendrix arguing has been made out to be a lot bigger deal than it actually was. In the end it was almost down to a flip of the coin. Let's face it The Who were a bloody hard act to follow at any time, but in all honesty I can't say that it bothered me.

Mitch, during the filming of a French T.V. show, May 1967.

The story of Townshend and Hendrix arguing has been made out to be a lot bigger deal than it actually was. In the end it was almost down to a flip of the coin. Let's face it The Who were a bloody hard act to follow at any time, but in all honesty I can't say that it bothered me.

Not advised for beginners! Jimi at Monterey, June 1967.

Monterey Festival, Monterey, California 18.6.67

Killing Floor; Foxy Lady; Like A Rolling Stone; Rock Me Baby; Hey Joe; Can You See Me; The Wind Cries Mary; Purple Haze; Wild Thing.
Note: A complete recording of this performance was made by Wally Heider at the soundboard and films of the festival include *Keep on Rocking* and *Monterey*.

The only time that the who-follows-who bit affected us was just a few weeks after Monterey at the Earl Warren Showgrounds in Santa Barbara, with Moby Grape, fine band – Jerry Miller a great guitar player – they insisted, or at least one of them did, that they were topping the bill and going to close the show. We said fine and went straight for the jugular – wasn't a lot left for them in the gig by the time we'd finished, plus we got off early for once and were able to get back to LA at a reasonable time.

Monterey for us was just amazing. Not only was it our first American gig, but the largest audience we'd ever played to. Paul McCartney, bless him, had recommended us to John Phillips for Monterey and we really wanted to deliver. I mean, just ten months before Jimi'd been playing in little clubs in New York, largely ignored.

There was a great atmosphere backstage, all the artists waiting in a huge marquee watching the show on monitors. We'd won the who-goes-last toss with The Who and stood watching them, waiting to go on. They were incredibly good as usual but we were too on-edge to enjoy it. When Pete Townsend broke up his guitar, which I seem to remember took quite a while, unusual for him – we thought, how do you top this? Mainly due to their excellence we decided that it was time to Roast-the-Fender again. This was only the second time Jimi had set fire to his guitar.

It seemed to take forever to get on stage but when we did, we just looked at each other and it was 'Lets go for it'. We really gave it everything and the set included Bob Dylan's 'Like A Rolling Stone' and of course 'Hey Joe'. We really enjoyed it, the audience were wonderful, they seemed to like us too.

When we came off stage drenched in sweat as usual, the other musicians and groups crowded round to congratulate us. That meant so much to us, *not only the audience approval but that of our peers as well.*

We'd done incredibly well in Europe in a very short time, we'd got to America, gone down really well. We thought we'd arrived. Boy, were we wrong. In the long term, of course, it was the best PR we could have possibly had, but we came out of that gig with *nothing*. I'm not just talking financially – we had no gigs. We were saved, basically by Bill Graham, who picked us up for the Fillmore, in San Francisco and by John Phillips who booked us to open for The Mamas & The Papas at the Hollywood Bowl.

BY THE TIME MONTEREY HAPPENED, SAN Francisco and its music scene were already international news and the phrase 'Summer of Love' was entering the language. Nothing comes from nothing and even the hippie culture of the Bay Area did not appear overnight at the drop of a tab of acid. The roots of the scene arguably dated right back to the days of the Gold Rush and the Barbary Coast, when the founding fathers of the City set a tone of tolerance that continues to the present day. In particular the 'new' culture grew out of the beatnik days of the Fifties, with writers like Jack Kerouac and Allen Ginsberg spending a great deal of time in the city, particularly in the North Beach area, famed for its coffee houses, jazz clubs and bookshops – notably Lawrence Ferlinghetti's City Lights store.

By the early Sixties the beatnik scene had waned, but radical and general counter-culture activity found new impetus through the folk-music revival. The new folk clubs rejuvenated North Beach as well as flowering in the suburban towns down the Peninsula, like Palo Alto and San Bruno. Most of the folk musicians hated the pop music of the era, but with the advent of the 'British Invasion' led by The Beatles in late 1964 they realized that electricity was OK. As a result many of the Bay Area folkies formed groups. Among them were Jerry Garcia who formed The Grateful Dead, Paul Kantner, The Jefferson Airplane and David Freiberg, Quicksilver Messenger Service. These 'first-generation' bands were all in existence by late 1965 and, although electric, they were still playing varying amounts of folk and standard R&B. Over the next year or so their music mutated into the eclectic hybrid dubbed the 'San Francisco Sound'.

Literally hundreds of similarly motivated bands sprang up in the Bay Area; at the same time Haight-Ashbury, a run-down district of the

city full of beautiful Victorian timber-framed houses, began to see a change of residents. At first it was just a few drop-outs from SF State College who settled there, but throughout 1966 Haight-Ashbury transformed itself into the largest hippie community in the States. Soon everybody under 21 wanted to go there. In theory every day was party-time; the reality for most was always a little different and by the summer of 1967, the area was swamped. Ironically, at the time when the world really

found out about the place, its glory days were essentially over, although a great deal of it, particularly the music, survived until the end of the decade.

The bands in San Francisco needed somewhere to play and the people needed somewhere to see them – and preferably be able to dance at the same time. As a result by early 1966, two major venues opened to cater for the music. The Avalon Ballroom, located at Sutter and Van Ness Streets, was the more community-

Janis Joplin and her band Big Brother and The Holding Company, 1967.

OPPOSITE: Jefferson Airplane, Jack Casady, (standing on the right, possibly in his pyjamas), was one of Jimi and Mitch's favourite bass players.

orientated and 'righteous' of the two. Run by genial Texan Chet Helms, the Avalon was the home-base for acts like Big Brother, Quicksilver Messenger Service and The Grateful Dead, but because of its readiness to stage benefits and generally help the community, it always teetered on the verge of bankruptcy and finally collapsed in late 1968.

By contrast the Fillmore Auditorium, at Fillmore and Geary, was, from the start, run with a greater degree of business acumen by Bill Graham. It too promoted many of the new bands and organized benefits. Graham was a music fan and put the music first but he was also financially shrewd, and although both ballrooms became famous, in the world at large it was the Fillmore that became inextricably linked with the San Francisco scene. If nothing else the greater cash-flow achieved by Graham enabled him to book visiting English groups like The Yardbirds and, of course, Hendrix.

We'd heard of the Fillmore, but nothing more. But thank God for Bill Graham, booking us in for six straight nights. We were staying down on Fisherman's Wharf in a hotel and they had Liberace's brother, George, playing violin in the lounge. That was always the thing to set you up before the gig – going down to see Brother George.

The original Fillmore bill was Gabor Szabo, us and The Airplane, but it was strange, poor old Gracie Slick, her voice went haywire after the first gig, just couldn't make it after that. I think that's why Big Brother with Janis ended up playing with us. Janis was just great. She had the hots for Gerry Stickells, our road manager. I remember her clearly jumping up and down on a hotel-room bed, her dog in one arm and a bottle of Southern Comfort in the other. We made some good friends through that gig, like the members of The Airplane, especially Jack Casady, the bass player. I got kidnapped on a couple of occasions and taken off to hear The Grateful Dead for what seemed like eight hours at a stretch.

On the Sunday afternoon before the last show we did a free concert on a flat bed truck in Golden Gate Park, really nice. I used Spencer Dryden of The Airplane's drums for the gig – thank you, Spencer.

After the week at the Fillmore we flew down to LA to hang out and pick up whatever gigs we could. We did a gig in Santa Barbara on July 1 and then the next night we opened for Sam and Dave at the Whiskey A Go-Go in LA. That was OK, we did all right considering it was their audience.

LEFT:
The Panhandle, San Francisco – A Sunday free concert, June 1967.

LEFT:
'Who turned on the lights?' Jimi, July 1967.

ABOVE:
Psychedelic concert
posters for two
California concerts,
(Santa Barbara and The
Fillmore), June 1967.

FROM LA THE BAND FLEW BACK TO NEW YORK – for an unspecified length of time, as there was no telling how many gigs that they might or might not pick up.

For some reason New York did not have an equivalent of the ballroom venues of San Francisco or Los Angeles. A couple of old theatres, the Village Theater and the Anderson Theater, put on occasional gigs, but the latter, at least, was considered cold and unfriendly. Later on there would be the Electric Circus and the Fillmore East (admittedly another theatre) but in mid 1967 the scene was still centred around the old folk clubs and cafés on Bleeker and

McDougal Streets in the Village. However, several of those like the Cafe Au Go-Go, the Cafe Wha! and the Night Owl had been featuring electric blues and folk rock bands like The Blues Project, The Lovin' Spoonful and The Magicians, for a couple of years. Some of the places, in fact, where Hendrix had played when he'd lived in New York.

As with London, there was another type of club – the up-market discotheque. Mostly they were uptown, places like Ondines and Cheetah, where Hendrix had occasionally played with Curtis Knight. By the time Hendrix returned, several more had opened or were about to do so.

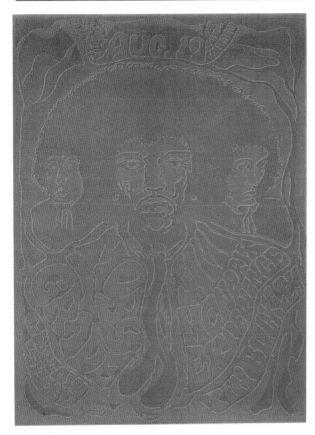

ABOVE:
Concert poster for the
Earl Warren
Showground Concert,
Santa Barbara, August
1967.

ABOVE:
'Unofficial' poster for the
Fillmore concert June
1967. Designed in
London by Hapshash
and The Coloured Coat.

Among the latter were The Salvation on Sheridan Square in the Village, at which The Experience played on its opening night in August (plus another four nights in the following week). But what was to become their home away from home and the first place they played in New York, was Steve Paul's Scene Club, on 46th Street, between Eighth and Ninth Avenues, near Times Square. Some of these places may have been sweaty dives, but like Blaises or the Bag o' Nails in London, it was really only the well-heeled hip élite who went to them.

The first thing we did in New York was the Scene Club. How we got that I don't know – maybe Chas knew Steve Paul, who ran it. It was a real sweaty armpit cellar, but an incredible audience, probably only held a couple of hundred people at most, legally. An amazing number of musicians would turn up there from Buddy Guy to Keith Jarrett, to Chuck Berry. A crazy mixture often on the same bill and often playing together. It became *the* place to go. I remember Albert King playing there one night. He had this ridiculously long guitar lead, 50 yards or even longer. He ended up playing out in the

Jimi, showing 'em how it's done.

Central Park, New York City, July 1967.

'Listen, guess what I've got for you, I've got this wonderful gig that you can't turn down. The tour of a lifetime . . . The Monkees.' We thought he was having us on. 'And you leave tomorrow!' We thought, 'Here we go again.' After The Walker Brothers and Engelbert, we get The Monkees.

Mitch, Central Park, New York City, July 1967.

street among the traffic . . . absolutely absurd.

Over the next year or so it was amazing for us – whenever we were in New York we lived between the hotel, the Record Plant and The Scene Club. The Scene became a watering-hole for musicians, particularly English bands. It was the first place we really encountered groupies on a mass scale. Hendrix used to call them Band-Aids. I've been asked many times if the debauchery didn't become boring. The answer is no – most entertaining. In America they seemed a lot more organised – shall I say professional. There was definitely a pecking-order there,

almost a union.

One thing that impressed me with Jimi, no matter where we were in the world, after we'd finished playing, we'd go out and check out whatever music was going on in town. Noel never wanted to come, preferring to stay in the hotel and listen to the Small Faces. If there was any chance of a play with other musicians, even better. Through Hendrix I got to play with some great musicians, although he did pull the odd stroke on me, but always with a great sense of fun.

Like one night we were in the Record Plant recording 'Electric Ladyland' and a

ABOVE RIGHT:
Mr. New York City –
July 1967.

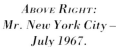

call comes in from Joe Tex, asking Jimi to come down and play at New York Town Hall.

Hendrix says, 'OK, but on one condition: I bring my drummer.' Tex agreed and Jimi says to me, 'Hey, come on, have a play with Joe Tex.'

I'm going, 'Yeah, I'll have some of that!'

So off we went in the limo, although it's only a couple of blocks to the gig. What he hadn't told me or maybe didn't know was that it was some kind of Black Power benefit – I'm the only white person there out of about four thousand people. Jimi chortling away, sort of, 'Ho ho, got the sucker now.'

So we get up on stage and there's all of Joe Tex's band up there – about seventeen of them – and the drums are set up out front. It was like, 'OK, sonny, let's see what you can do!' I had to deal with it or get the hell out. So I did the best I could and it was OK. I wouldn't have missed it for the world.

Anyway we were still in New York looking for gigs and at some point Chas received a phone call from Mike Jeffery, God knows where from. We only ever saw Jeffery about twice in the first year, any of us. You never knew what he was up to or where he was. Anyway Chas got the call, 'Listen, guess what I've got you. I've got this wonderful gig that you can't turn down. The tour of a lifetime . . . The Monkees.'

We thought he was having us on.

'And you leave tomorrow!'

We thought, 'Here we go again.' After The Walker Brothers and Engelbert, we get The Monkees.

Basically The Monkees were trying to outdo The Beatles. Everything, but everything, was paid for by Screen Gems, I'd never been exposed to anything like it.

They were a nice bunch of chaps, even though we thought they couldn't play. We shared the private plane and all that, but God, did their audience hate us. Eight-year-old kids with their mums and dads, no wonder they hated us. We opened in Jacksonville and as I said before, that tour was our first experience of the South and racism.

I remember that first gig: we opened up and the house lights were still on and people were still filing into their seats. Could have been Tom and Jerry on stage, they didn't care. So Hendrix tried to baffle them with volume, just trying to make some kind of impression. We just wanted out basically, so Chas had words with Dick Clarke the promoter and then the whole 'Daughters of the American Revolution' hype – that is that we were corrupting their wholesome children – was dreamed up afterwards. I don't think any of it was true but some people had complained and it got us off the tour, so I guess it was OK.

There were some nice things about the tour. We did a couple of days on Greyhound buses and we discovered that Peter Tork could play banjo, Mike Nesmith could play guitar, Mickey Dolenz was one hell of a nice guy and Davy Jones was extremely short.

I had my 21st birthday on the tour, the second day in fact, and we were on board the private plane at Jacksonville about to travel to Miami for the second gig. Several bottles of champagne had been broken out in my honour and as we were taxiing, the wing hit the sign on the top of one of those Shell petrol pumps. You think that they are just signs, or at least I did. Wrong! This thing had flames coming out of it! I'm feeling no pain by this stage, I'm going, 'Look, fireworks for my birthday.' Anyway it was OK and the flight was fine, fun had by all. Very nice way to spend my birthday I thought.

The next day before the gig – I think we were playing the Jackie Gleason Memorial Hall in Miami – we were taken out on these boats around the inland waterways. All part of The Monkees touring party. The other thing about that was that Jimi was the only person I've ever seen wear a fur coat in 90-degree weather.

The gigs all in all were OK, but by about the third day Davy Jones really started getting on our nerves. Noel, at some point, discovered he had an amyl nitrate capsule which he claimed belonged to his grandmother for her heart condition. He broke it under Davy Jones nose, who passed out on the floor. A sight to behold.

I'm glad we did the tour as it was something I would never have experienced otherwise. We lasted for five gigs, the last of which was a couple of nights at Forest Hills near New York, where they *really* hated us. This surprised us a bit as we'd already done a gig in Central Park, just prior to the tour, supporting The Young Rascals and gone down really well. But, no they hated us. They didn't exactly throw things, but it was fairly hostile – especially the mums and dads.

Just before leaving on the tour we did our

first US recording, at Mayfair, with Gary Kellagran. We cut 'Midnight Lamp' certainly and probably 'The Stars That Play With Laughing Sam's Dice' the B-side, although we may have done that after we'd finished the tour.

I remember I got a new drum kit for the tour and the 'Midnight Lamp' session was the first time I used them. Mayfair was a tiny studio, just by Times Square, about eight flights up. Tiny, but a great sound and Gary Kellagran was an excellent engineer. He was basically the reason we ended up at the Record Plant, since that was where he moved on to. The song 'The Stars That Played with Laughing Sam's Dice' was a deliberate joke, you know, S.T.P. and L.S.D. But it was just a filler, done in one take with the background vocals done by people in the studio. They were mainly Jimi's

Mitch, Mayfair Studios, New York City, July 1967.

old friends like Devon Wilson. Although LSD was taken by all of us for recreational purposes back then, there is really nothing to be read into the song. Just a quickly written B-side, so needless to say it was never done on stage.

We managed a few gigs in New York after the tour. We opened a new club called the Salvation down in the Village – nice place, but not designed for rock 'n' roll and we did at least a couple of nights at the Cafe Au Go Go. I remember that because Zappa and The Mothers were in the upstairs bit, the Garrick Theater, this being during their six-month residency. I sat in with them once and I think

Jimi may well have too, I'm not sure.

Going back to New York was obviously a big deal for Jimi, as it was for all of us. I had no real idea what to expect. I was so naive, I phoned up to make a reservation to see Elvin Jones, one of the finest jazz drummers in the world, playing at this little club in the Village. I went down expecting it to be full and there was no one there at all, I couldn't believe it.

We weren't living in luxury and gigs were still thin on the ground but it must have been a big deal for Jimi to go back after all that time scuffling around in the Village in those sleazy clubs. Must have been quite some

Jimi, at the Cafe au Go-Go, New York City, July 1967. Harvey Brookes on bass and Buddy Miles on drums.

ABOVE:
Jimi and unidentified friends atop Rudolph Valentino's mansion, California 1967.

ABOVE:
Beverly Hillbilly – Mitch in Hollywood, 1967.

LEFT:
A rare outdoors shot of Jimi, Hyde Park, London, 1969.

BELOW:
Papas without their Mamas. (l) Denny Dogherty and (r) John Phillips, Hollywood Bowl, 1967.

LEFT:
Noel Redding, bass player for the Jimi Hendrix Experience till end of June 1969.

RIGHT:
Mama Cass in curlers, rehearsing at the Hollywood Bowl, 1967.

BELOW LEFT:
Mitch camouflaged for California, 1967.

BELOW RIGHT:
Jimi, in a Swedish hotel room, 1968.

The 'Guitar-In' at the Festival Hall, London. Looking slightly out-of-place with Jimi's guitar is politician Jeremy Thorpe.

change. He would disappear from time to time, but mainly he would have people come over to the hotel.

Hendrix was really suited to hotel life and night life. Noel and I called him 'The Bat'. He would get into his room, close the curtains, put coloured silk scarves over all the lamps, get the guitars out, and he was completely at home. When we started to spend more time in New York, I made a conscious decision to move out and get a hotel away from it all. What was incredible though, and I think it's something people overlook, is that it was only ten months since Jimi had left New York with nothing and there he was back there, a celebrity. I would like to think that even without the foresight of Chas, Jimi would have made it ultimately,

but there is always that doubt. So much of it was a matter of alchemy, timing, luck or whatever. I mean if I hadn't have been fired on that Monday, I possibly wouldn't have gone to that audition the next day.

THE LAST PHASE OF THE EXPERIENCE'S FIRST American visit started with five nights at the Ambassador Theater in Washington. The gig was memorable, at least for Mitch, since he missed the second night due to a suspected appendicitis – the only time he missed a gig with Hendrix that he was booked to play. After Washington they did a one-off gig at the Fifth Dimension club in either Ann Arbor or Detroit (Mitch can't remember which) and then down to LA for a final couple of days. While there they did gigs in Santa Barbara with Moby Grape and

GUITAR - IN

The Jimi Hendrix Experience

Bert Jansch   Paco Pena

Sebastian Jorgensen and Tim Walker

THE ROYAL FESTIVAL HALL

8 p.m., Monday, 25th September

Tickets: 21/-, 15/6, 12/6, 7/6, 5/-

Available from the Royal Festival Hall box office (telephone 01-928 3191)

The Mamas & The Papas at the Hollywood Bowl.

Our other major West Coast gig was the Hollywood Bowl as guests of The Mamas & The Papas. For Noel and I, particularly, it was like, 'Cor, the Hollywood Bowl. The Beatles played there.' They were all incredibly friendly towards us, nice gig, but again it wasn't our crowd. The word was going round LA about us, but the audience had booked their seats months before to see them, not us. We went down OK, but nothing grand.

Great party afterwards at Phillips's mansion in Bel Air, quite extraordinary meeting Steve McQueen and people like that. Our first real Hollywood affair. We'd already met several of the LA musicians like David Crosby and Peter Tork, of course, and had been to Stephen Stills's place out in Malibu. That's where the jamming thing really started for Jimi and me. At Stills's place the equipment was up 24 hours for anybody that dropped by.

After the Hollywood Bowl gig we had to come back to England. I got arrested at the airport for having a gas gun that I'd bought round the corner from the White House. I just bought it as a souvenir and I was duly relieved of it. They took no further action, but I used to be given a hard time leaving England in the early days.

In those days there were currency restrictions and you weren't allowed to take out more than a certain amount of money per year, something stupid like 40 pounds. We were leaving about three times a week at one stage – going to France for TV for a day,

ABOVE:
Jimi with Mama Cass backstage at the Saville Theatre, London, October 1967.

BELOW:
Future Fender flambé? France, 1967.

Jimi at Monterey, California, June 1967.

coming back, going to Sweden the next day. I got stopped five times in two weeks. I would have ten bob (8 cents) over and I'd say, 'Look, give it to the Widows Pension Fund or something,' and they would refuse and take me back and insist that I paid it into an account. It was harassment, basically. We did put a complaint in and eventually a few knuckles were rapped, but it was a pain in the arse. They didn't bother Hendrix too

much, possibly because he had an American passport.

I had mixed feelings about coming back from the States, even that first time. I'd begun to get the flavour of it, especially LA. I'd never seen anything like it at all. There was still work to do in Europe, but it was really a question of honouring bookings and getting some recording done. We knew we'd be back sooner rather than later. I must admit I wouldn't have minded a few more months over there at that time. Noel wasn't homesick exactly, but I think he was quite pleased to go back.

It was pretty much back to what we'd done before, including another Swedish tour in the September. I think it was in Stockholm that we turned up at the hotel and there's a red carpet laid out, people were giving us lots of help to carry our baggage in. We thought, 'Hey, this is great,' thinking it was meant for us. In fact they were trying to get rid of us because Princess Alexandra and her husband were coming in and we were holding them up.

After Sweden, we played this thing at the Festival Hall, called the Guitar-In. I don't remember the other players, but it was a workshop sort of thing with mainly classical musicians, apart from us. I remember Jeremy Thorpe, then leader of the Liberal Party, turned up and had all those photos taken. All those great shots of him having his hair teased by Hendrix and holding the flying V guitar. Again not our sort of crowd, I think Princess Margaret was there – a lot of people with fingers in ears. A nice gig for us to play, nonetheless.

We were still doing the odd club gig in England like the Boathouse in Nottingham, which was strange after Monterey and the Hollywood Bowl. We were really just honouring old commitments, which every newly successful act had to go through. I remember reading that The Beatles, when they were at No. 1 had a contract for something stupid like sixty pounds.

Just after the Guitar-In we spent three days in Paris. We did the usual Olympia gigs on October 10, then the next day or the day after, we did another one of our early-morning filming sessions, on some kind of building site. The difference was that we did a live version of the 'Marseillaise'. The story I've heard is that the French government were so appalled by this desecration, that the film was seized and, if it survives at all, is locked in a government vault.

Mitch, Noel and Jimi backstage at the Olympia, Paris, October 1967.

The J.H.E. posing for French television, October 1967.

INSET RIGHT: The Experience arrive back in London after their first tour of America, August, 1967.

RIGHT: Jimi performing in London, December 1967.

BY THIS TIME THE BAND HAD STARTED WORK on their second album, 'Axis: Bold As Love'. As before, recording dates were sandwiched in between gigs, and the album – though relatively quickly produced in terms of studio hours – was not completed until the end of October. The completed album was a more textured and produced affair than 'Experienced', reflecting the growing split between the 'Experience-on-stage' captured on the first album and an increasing desire to produce something different in the studio. None the less several tracks were already – or later became – on-stage favourites, notably 'Spanish Castle Magic' and 'Little Wing'. Under Chas's watchful eye and with the relatively primitive equipment at Olympic, the actual method of production was not that different from before.

By this time we'd started work on our second album. We didn't approach 'Axis' that differently from the first one, although it didn't seem to be as much of a rush. There was a fair amount of material already there to be done, but as usual a lot of stuff got tried out in the studio and it either clicked or it didn't. 'Experienced' was very much, 'Wham, bam, thank you – next track'; 'Axis: Bold As Love' was like that as well to a degree – if only because there was pressure on us to produce a good follow-up – but much less so.

From my side I felt happy to be in a studio, particularly Olympic. Working on 'Axis' was the first time that it became apparent that Jimi was pretty good working behind the board, as well as playing and had some positive ideas of how he wanted things recorded. It could have been the start of any potential conflict between him and Chas in the studio. Chas was fair, though, and realized that Hendrix knew what he was doing and that there were engineers, like Eddie Kramer – who were among the first to experiment with phasing or flanging sound – who could really improve things. It was about that time that I realized that Hendrix could play something forwards and know exactly how it would sound if it was played back in reverse. An amazing facility.

Where tempers did start to get a little frayed was over re-takes. Chas was quite happy for layers of overdubs and effects to be put on a track, but he tried to draw the line over simply doing more and more takes of the same thing. All he could see was the budget going up and up all the time. Noel really didn't like spending that much time in the studio, especially doing take after take. Often it got to the point where he would go over the road to the pub. When that happened Jimi and I would often continue without him, which was no big deal really. We would lay down guitar and drums or bass and drums, but usually it meant that Noel could come in later and add his bass part. Not that unusual, standard recording procedure really.

Jimi was helped a lot by Roger Meyer, who'd basically invented fuzzboxes and given them to Jeff Beck and Jimmy Page. He started developing equipment specifically for Jimi, to enable him to produce the sounds he wanted. On the first album neither Noel nor I had any say in how we actually sounded. We laid down our tracks and that was it; Chas recorded it and mixed it virtually alone. Even Jimi only had a limited say – he knew the overall sound he wanted but ultimately what Chas said went.

Listening to it now, I think that Chas did an extremly good job, with the equipment and facilities available. But by the second album, Jimi had started to find his own feet and Noel and I wanted some kind of impact with regards to our sound. Chas did his best to put up with us, which can't have been easy. I think he and Jimi were still sharing a flat together and consequently living in each others' pockets. I think that's going to lead to strain in any relationship.

The strain was certainly showing between the band and Chas by the time we did the track, 'Bold As Love'. I particularly wanted to go for this flanging sound on the drums and finish the album with something quite big and impressive. That took a long, long time to set up in the studio. Chas's patience definitely started wearing thin, but we were allowed to do it.

Axis: Bold as Love LP sleeve.

AXIS: BOLD AS LOVE Track 613 003 (12.67)
US Reprise RS 6281

SIDE 1   EXP; Up From The Skies; Spanish Castle Magic; Wait Until Tomorrow; Ain't No Telling; Little Wing; If Six Was Nine.
SIDE 2   You've Got Me Floating; Castles Made Of Sand; She's So Fine; One Rainy Wish; Little Miss Lover; Bold As Love.

All titles written by Jimi Hendrix except 'She's So Fine' which is by Noel Redding.
Produced by Chas Chandler. Engineered by Eddie Kramer.

Poster for the Saville Theatre, designed by Hapshash and the Coloured Coat.

Jimi outside his flat in Montagu Square 1967. The previous tenant was one Ringo Starr.

It was first time I actually got to sit at the board and work on my drum sound. It didn't go down too well, but Jimi really stuck by me. Lots of musicians dropped by our recording sessions, one of whom was Brian Jones. Jimi always had a very soft spot for Brian. I don't know how they first met, probably through Brian coming to some of our early gigs, like the 7½ Club or wherever. They'd see each other quite a lot, but musically there was no great interaction, Brian would go back to Jimi's place occasionally or vice versa, strum a few guitars here and there, but on stage – never.

However, the Stones were working in

ABOVE:
Filming session at the Roundhouse, London late '67.

*Rock 'n' Roll Circus –
John Lennon, Eric
Clapton, Keith Richards
and Mitch Mitchell,
December 1968.*

Olympic, normally from three in the afternoon till nine o'clock at night. We would come in at nine and on a couple of occasions Brian was either late for their sessions or had nothing to do on them, so he dropped in on us. He would pull out various exotic instruments and play along with us, while the equipment was being set up. I've heard sitar mentioned, but I don't think so. It was fun, but nothing really gelled and no serious recording was ever attempted. Jimi remained friends with Brian right up until Brian's death, which, I think, hit Jimi really hard.

One thing that came of this situation was Mick Jagger asking me to play in the Rock 'n' Roll Circus. I did, playing with Eric Clapton, Keith Richards and John Lennon – a film exists which the Stones are sitting on and I don't think it's seen the light of day yet. Keith played bass and was great at *that* as well. Eric Clapton was on guitar – who could ask for more? Both were great favourites of Jimi's and mine, as was John Lennon. We played John's song 'Yer Blues'. Though I was a long-time admirer, this was the first time I'd played with Lennon who really delivered the goods. Great voice, great rhythm guitar – I hope he enjoyed it as much as I did.

BELOW:
The Jimi Hendrix Experience and Arthur Brown 1967.

BELOW RIGHT:
Programme for a 'package tour' with Pink Floyd and others, November 1967.

In mid-November, the band was booked on another package tour – one might have thought that the management had learned by now. At least this time the band were in the company of groups with a similar musical attitude. The line-up Pink Floyd, The Nice, Amen Corner, The Move and The Experience

were all, with the exception of Amen Corner, loosely associated with, if not actually part of, the Underground. They'd all, with the exception of The Nice, had hits, so someone somewhere must have thought, 'Hey, these guys sell records, better put them on a tour.' Of course, the idea was in some ways more ludicrous than the standard pop tour; they were, after all, still limited to the usual 15–30 minute sets, just time for about one Pink Floyd number!

By late 1967 most people regarded the package tour as a dinosaur and this tour may well have helped to put it in the grave.

In a way the tour was more absurd than the previous one, because *none* of the bands on this one was package-tour material. The line-up was Amen Corner, The Move, Pink Floyd, The Nice and us. It was actually good fun – lunacy most of the time, however. Syd Barrett, who was still with Pink Floyd, didn't talk to anyone during that time. In fact David Gilmour, who was ultimately Syd's 'replacement' joined the tour halfway through.

At Sophia Gardens in Cardiff there is film of Noel riding across the stage on a bike, with me chasing him with a whip, during The

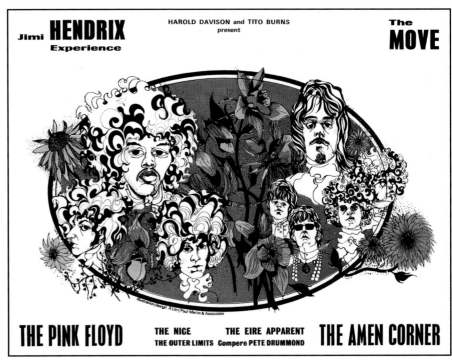

Move's set. Sheer madness, it was that sort of tour. It was still the standard package tour, short sets and stuff, but at least by that time it was our sort of audience.

THE LAST GIG OF 1967 FOR THE EXPERIENCE, was the 'Christmas on Earth Continued' event held on December 22 at London's Olympia exhibition hall. It was a huge event, rivalling the earlier, '14 Hour Technicolor Dream' (at which The Experience hadn't performed) and featured – apart from The Experience, who headlined – The Who, Eric Burdon And The Animals, Pink Floyd and many others. With a fairground and film shows, the idea was obviously to create a multi-media happening and to some extent it worked. Some people regard it as the last great British Underground event, others see it as a commercial cash-in. It's well worth noting that two numbers from Hendrix's

set turned up on the video of The Experience's performance at Monterey. Where the film of the rest of the set (and indeed of the other performers) resides is currently unknown.

I remember that Olympia gig really well. In the afternoon they had this huge inflatable cushion which they intended to use as a prop and while they were blowing it up a few of us decided to sit on it. It was the size of a mini swimming pool and the top was about eight feet off the ground when it was fully inflated. Somehow I managed to lose my grip and slipped off it hitting my head really hard on the concrete floor. Looking back I should have gone and had it checked out, because I was definitely concussed. I didn't mention it to anybody and played the gig, but it was one of the few times when I really felt uncomfortable playing.

LEFT:
J.H.E. rehearsing for 'Christmas on Earth Continued', an all-night pop concert, December, 1967.

RIGHT AND ABOVE:
Mitch, Jimi and Noel rehearsing for the Royal Albert Hall, London, November 1967.

Poster advertising the all-night pop festival at Olympia, London, 1967.

when maybe Jimi had inadvertently taken something before playing. There was one time in Germany when he couldn't tune up properly and Noel had to do it. We stumbled through a few numbers and had to cancel the gig. Normally though he was a real trooper and the show must go on and all that, let's go on and do it. After the show we would indulge in a bit of recreation and things could be a little different, but no great shakes.

One thing we had noticed was that he never drank very much at all, but that if he did drink, especially whisky, it affected him badly. Anyway we were in Gothenburg, had done the concert and gone back to the hotel, nothing unusual. There was the usual thing of people knocking on your door, including, obviously Hendrix's. For whatever reason he'd been drinking that night and he lost his rag with someone trying to get into his room. We heard this commotion out on the landing and myself, Noel and Gerry Stickells appeared to see what was going on and calm things down.

I took Jimi back into my room – whereupon he started trying to smash things up, which didn't go down too well with me. Somehow we struggled with him and got him out into the corridor again, I think I then threw a very feeble punch at him, which amazed him rather than anything else. We then got him on to the floor and managed to sit on him. Unfortunately, he'd smashed a plate-glass window in my room and the police were called, who promptly arrested him.

In some ways it was the best thing that could have happened. Not for Jimi really, but we'd been working solidly without a break for over a year and were totally knackered. In court they fined him and made him pay for the window – no big deal – also they made him stay in Sweden, on probation for a week.

It was probably just what the guy needed. 'Hell, this is going to be really rough for me, a week off in Sweden.' We couldn't get a flight out, because the airport was snowed in and it took us two and a half days to get back by ferry to England.

The first gigs of 1968 were in Sweden again, another mini-tour that produced the first problems we ever had with Jimi. There had been a couple of things before that,

RIGHT:
Jimi at the film première
of 'How I Won the War'
1967.

BELOW:
The J.H.E. with
members of The Soft
Machine, December
1967.

HAVE CONTRACT, MUST TRAVEL

IN FEBRUARY 1968 THE EXPERIENCE WENT BACK to the States for their first proper tour, although like the first visit the tour grew as it went on, dates being added on all the time, until the band were essentially living on the road in America. After the first few dates, The Experience were joined by The Soft Machine and slightly later by The Eire Apparent, both managed by The Experience's co-manager, the ubiquitous Mike Jeffery. It was a long and gruelling tour, but if it did nothing else it established The Experience as one of the leading rock acts of the day.

We went back to America in February 1968, with The Soft Machine and at some stage, The Eire Apparent. An all-Mike Jeffery package. I didn't know The Soft Machine too well at that stage. I'd seen them at the UFO club in London and I'd met them in the Gerrard Street office a few times, and I liked them and their music, but that was about it. As the tour progressed I got to know them, particularly Mike Ratledge, the keyboard player and Robert Wyatt, the drummer. Robert, in fact, put me on to people like Cecil Taylor who I wouldn't have heard otherwise. I know Hendrix thought very highly of them – a great band.

Night after night they never lost their impetus. It was always a challenge to them, especially some places in the Mid-West, where it wasn't really their audience. They were a hard act to follow, every night. We were doing two shows a night on the tour and had to get up at seven o'clock in the morning.

It wasn't quite thrust down our throats, but it was made clear to us that we were lucky to be travelling by plane. Hendrix never said much about it, because he'd been raised on doing the Greyhound bus circuit, all over America. Every other English band up to us, I suppose, had done that as well. Not many people were flying around. I suppose it was luxury of a sort. However, after doing a gig and being a silly lad partying all night and getting an hour's sleep, to be woken up at seven with a plane to catch didn't go down too well.

I had a routine of checking into a hotel and taking these two great big bolts with me, which I would attach to the door. I then took the phone off the hook. Frequently they had to call the fire brigade to break down the door to get me up, but it did get the flight times altered. It was ridiculous: on the first half of that tour with The Soft Machine we did over 40 cities in under 50 days.

I don't think that The Soft Machine did the first couple of gigs on that tour with us, but they were certainly on the bill for the February 10 show at the Shrine in LA. In the

RIGHT:
Mitch on second J.H.E.
tour of America (with
The Soft Machine)
Hollywood, February
1968.

FAR RIGHT:
Jimi, early 1968, on tour
in America.

88

It was ridiculous: on the first half of that tour with The Soft Machine we did over 40 cities in under 50 days.

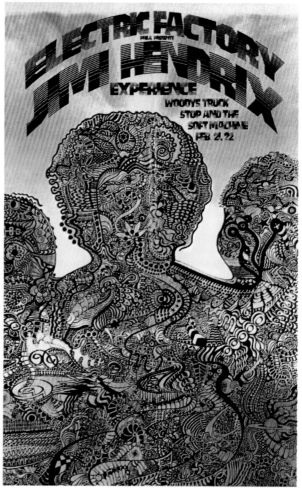

Above:
Poster for tour with The Soft Machine, 1968.

Left:
Modern 20th Anniversary reprint of original Coliseum poster.

Three American posters advertising the second Jimi Hendrix Experience tour (with Soft Machine), 1968.

afternoon we'd gone to open a record store, next to where the Pandora's Box club had been, right by where Laurel Canyon starts. They'd made giant JIMI HENDRIX EXPERIENCE posters that covered the entire frontage of the store – it really looked quite impressive.

We'd heard a rumour about this other band who were on the bill that night, called Blue Cheer. They were going to 'blow us off the stage'. Oh, really? Lots of amps and all that, but what a piece of shit. Outside of The Seeds, who we worked with in the Scene in New York, we thought they were one of the worst fucking bands we'd ever heard.

The next day we played in Seattle, Jimi's home town, of course. I'm not sure how long it had been since he'd last been there or seen his folks – several years, certainly. I know that going back had been on his mind for a while and he was probably a little apprehensive about it. Anyway they met us at the airport, lovely family, father a charming man. He'd remarried at some point and there were all these really beautiful girls, who were Jimi's new relatives. I remember him saying, 'Oh, you're my sister? Really?' My opinion was, 'Keep it out of the family, very nice to meet you.' Al, Jimi's Dad, was obviously delighted to see his son and genuinely pleased that he'd made good. We all went over to Al's place in the afternoon and then after the gig Jimi went back to spend the evening with them. He and Al got through a bottle of whisky and, oh dear, was the boy ill next morning.

I think it was the second time in Seattle that Jimi was asked to go back to his old school, Garfield High – from which he'd been more or less thrown out – to speak at the morning assembly. I remember him talking about it the day before and he really didn't

BELOW:
The J.H.E. in America, Mitch doing his Laurel & Hardy impression, 1968.

RIGHT:
Jimi moving in for the kill, early 1968.

want to do it, although he could see the humour of it. He went through with it, but at nine in the morning after another night of whisky!

Jimi was undoubtedly a very, very, funny man, certainly not the tragic figure certain people have made him out to be. He had a wonderful sense of humour and was one of the best mimics I've ever heard. He did a fabulous Nat King Cole doing, 'Rambling Rose' and a pretty mean Sammy Davis Jnr as well. He also did really funny drawings. It's difficult to describe now but believe me he was one of the funniest people I've ever known.

After Seattle we did a show at the University of California, Los Angeles. The performance itself was nothing exceptional but backstage the Warner/Reprise rep. introduced us to this reed-thin, really ill-looking person, who turned out to be none other than Alice Cooper. It scared the hell out of us – he'd just been passed A1 physically fit for the draft. We thought, 'If this guy's healthy, what chance do we stand?' Later on I did get a draft notice, because I was spending more than six months of the year in the States. In fact I was sent by the office to Canada for the day; I never knew why until years later when I was told that it was to get round my draft notice which finally arrived. Could equally have been bullshit of course.

Thinking of Vietnam, it's amazing how many vets have come up to me in America – great big blokes you think are going to start a fight – but no, they just want to tell you how much our music meant to them in Vietnam and say thanks. Jimi would have been really proud – that would have meant a lot to him.

The next stage of the tour was Texas – first time we'd been there. I think we did four days there – San Antonio, Dallas, Fort Worth and Houston, something like that. We were assigned one security guard for all four days. This typical big, burly, easy-going Texan made sure we weren't hassled too much – a nice guy. He drove us around and generally looked after us.

On the last day, the Sunday, he turned up

LEFT:
Jimi, tuning up in the dressing room, somewhere in America, 1968.

RIGHT:
Jimi in London, 1968.

in full *police* uniform. He's like the Chief of Police for most of Texas – we'd had no idea. Various substances had been smoked, there were young women around and he's a cop. We really weren't sure what to do.

Anyway, before the first show on the Sunday, Noel and I figured we'd get some food and a couple of beers. Not possible – the whole place was dry on Sunday. So we asked the only person we could, our friend the policeman, to help us out. Much to our amazement he said, 'Whatever you want, boys,' and promptly phoned the Mayor. Within an hour everything we wanted turned up.

I think the tour moved on to Philadelphia after that – two nights at the Electric Factory. Quite bizarre, that was the era of body painting and people coming on stage and 'doing their thing, man', whether you wanted them there or not. The whole psychedelia thing had spread right over America, or the cosmopolitan bits of it at least, and the Electric Factory was like a Philadelphia version of the Fillmore. Mind you, it was spreading to, if not exactly hick towns, then certainly more conservative ones. We'd been through some on the first tour of the States and they were totally straight-laced and we'd come back not that much later and find that things had definitely changed. The message, whatever it was, was certainly spreading.

Because we were travelling so much we never really knew what was going on unless it smacked you in the face – like the body painters in Philadelphia. So we didn't really know which towns were fairly loose and tolerant and those that weren't.

At some point one of the roadies decided that rather than obtain our grass locally whenever we arrived somewhere, we would carry our own with us. At one time we must have had a kilo and half with us. Normally this was OK, but sometimes you'd be sitting with some locals and you'd pull out the dope and they'd be amazed, 'Christ, don't you know what it's like in this town?' We'd go, 'Whoops, er no, no, we don't.' I'd beat a hasty retreat on those occasions. In some

places not only did the neighbourhood police have it in for the local radicals, but also for two white boys and a black appearing together, especially if we were seen to be indulging ourselves with the local women.

Wherever you were it was always watch your step time, but some places were better than others. San Francisco was never a problem, LA was variable, especially when the authorities had the curfew on the kids; New York was fine in terms of the police, it was just cabs and hotels that were a problem. In Texas we always knew we'd have a lot of fun, but anywhere else was potentially threatening.

Obviously, we played a lot of towns more than once and I'm not sure on which visits certain things happened, but I think it was on this tour in Detroit, right after the Philadelphia gigs, that we nearly got shot. I think we heard on the TV as we were leaving the hotel, 'There's been a problem with snipers today in downtown Detroit da da da', and we walked out through the revolving doors and we can hear all these ricocheting bullets, some of them really close, and we had to make a dash for the car. It was the first time that I felt that my safety was really threatened.

After Detroit we played Toronto and I think it was that night, that after our gig we sat in with Robbie Robertson and some of the guys from The Hawks, later, of course, The Band. It was one of those after-hours things in a small club.

What was played on those after-hours sessions varied from night to night. Sometimes we just played things we all knew, sometimes it was more complex things – usually it was a bit of both. Generally if you heard a band and they were playing 'Suzie Q' or whatever and you liked the sound and the style, you'd just try to slide in to the background and play as they did, it was their band, after all. It wasn't a case of a take-over bid. Although, by that stage, with Hendrix, you got the inevitable thing of, 'Guess who we've got in the audience tonight?' Generally he would have preferred just to have merged in – he always made his

The J.H.E. listing to the left at the Beverly Hills Hotel, February 1968.

presence felt anyway. He never went out to intentionally razzle-dazzle an audience on his time off, or to steal anyone else's limelight.

After Toronto I certainly do remember what happened the next night. We were in Chicago, playing the Opera House and for some reason the gig was at a ridiculous time, like three in the afternoon – and only one show, for a change. We played, got the limo back to the hotel, usual thing and it's, 'What are we gonna do tonight?'

'Well, we can always go to the South Side to hear some blues.' But that wouldn't start till about one in the morning, plus it was

The Smash Hits album. Enhanced for stereo from original mono recordings.

SMASH HITS (Compilation) Track 613 004 (4.68) US Reprise MS 2025

SIDE 1 Purple Haze; The Wind Cries Mary; Can You See Me; 51st Anniversary; Hey Joe; Stone Free.
SIDE 2 The Stars That Play With Laughing Sam's Dice; Manic Depression; Highway Chile; Burning Of The Midnight Lamp; Foxy Lady.

All Titles written by Jimi Hendrix except 'Hey Joe' which is by Billy Roberts. Produced by Chas Chandler.

Sunday, as well. The whole place would probably be closed. Anyway we got out of the car and this other car, which had been tailing ours, screeched in front of us.

These three girls got out, each holding a Samsonite brief case and presented us with their cards. 'I see you are the er Plaster Casters and oh, you do that, do you? . . . Hmm.' We had, in fact, heard of them, from Eric Burdon, I think. He'd told us about these women who do vile things with parts of your body, if you let them. 'Oh, yeah, fine, Eric. Yawn.'

Anyway they somehow got invited up to one of the rooms to, shall I say, demonstrate their art. The one thing I should mention is that they hadn't really perfected the process at the time – the moulding technique, dare I say. If one is plunging parts of one's anatomy into a vase filled up with dental casting alginate, it may be pleasurable for some, but for others it can leave a lot to be desired, and to retain that position while the stuff sets is quite difficult, I'm led to believe.

Apart from that there is the problem of extracting oneself afterwards, when certain parts of the anatomy might stick. I understand that several trial runs had to be made before they perfected things. I have to say, in all fairness to them, that they were serious and professional people.

After that we did some weird gigs in the Mid-West, places like Madison and Milwaukee. I don't remember much about them except that one turned out to be organized by one of the East Coast 'Families'. Around this time, though, we actually managed three days off, so I flew to the Bahamas with a girlfriend. Noel joined us, which was odd because he really doesn't like sunshine, beyond the odd hour lying by the pool. He gave it all of three hours, whereupon he decided he hated the Bahamas and flew straight back again.

Needless to say the tour continued after we returned, but the only gig that stands out was the Cleveland Music Hall at the end of March. Serious business that one. We had a lot of problems with the unions on the first show, 'You can't move that,' etc., upsetting

Jimi, performing mid-tour, 1968.

We got out of the car and this other car, which had been tailing ours, screeched in front of us. These three girls got out, each holding a Samsonite brief case and presented us with their cards. 'I see you are the er Plaster Casters and oh, you do that, do you.'

ABOVE:
One of the best engineers around in the 60's – Gary Kellegran – who worked with the J.H.E. at Mayfair Studios and The Record Plant.

RIGHT:
Lay back and groove . . .

the roadies no end. We had to make the usual pay-off to the Teamsters and their mothers and their second cousins once removed. In the afternoon Jimi and Noel went out with Mike Goldstein, our publicist at the time. He was a local lad and knew the neighbourhood car dealers, so he took Noel and Jimi out to order their first cars – it was the first time we'd actually had any money to spend. So Jimi ordered a Stingray and Noel, I think, ordered a Mercury Cougar, which he never took delivery of.

At the second show there was a bomb threat – I think they found 'a suspicious package' and they cleared the hall. Who exactly was responsible for it we never did find out.

A couple of days later we were back in Chicago, at Xavier University. It was a strange hall, a bit like the Hollywood Bowl but indoors and at the back of the stage was this metal sheeting. There was a radio station on campus, close by and their signal bounced off the metal sheeting, so you got all kinds of shit feeding through the amps. It really pissed me off, because that day I'd been to the Ludwig drum factory – they'd given me the guided tour and I picked up a great big, brand new bass drum. I was really looking forward to playing it – 'You wait till the boys hear this!' And of course we get there and didn't get beyond one number – blew my evening.

By this time we were playing 60-minute shows, maybe 75 with encores. Don't forget, though, that we were doing two shows a night, plus the after-hours stuff, plus the travelling. I doubt whether we'd have wanted to do much more. The shows were always formatted to an extent, you had to, with maybe three acts and two complete shows. But it was never the same twice. Some numbers, say 'Sgt. Pepper's', might be twenty minutes long one night and three the next and we had a large repertoire, so we didn't have to do the same numbers every night. A lot depended on how we felt and what we got from the audience.

Audience reaction was important, but it could have a negative effect. They may have

ABOVE:
Mitch in the studio, the Record Plant, New York City, 1968.

been on their feet, yelling and screaming, but if all they wanted was for Jimi to burn the guitar or whatever, it could be a real turn-off. Equally, if they were sitting more or less in silence, did it mean that they were listening or were they simply not enjoying it? We were usually quick to pick that up, but it did vary every night. I mean some nights we just didn't play too well and the next would be great. So many things could affect it.

101

Jimi relaxing in Canada, 1968.

Burning Of The Midnight Lamp/The Stars That Play With Laughing Sam's Dice Track 604 007 (8.67)

Voodoo Chile/Watchtower Polydor 2121 012 (10.68) (This is the German version which was backed by All Along The Watchtower)

All Along The Watchtower/Long Hot Summer Night Track 604 025 (10.68)

Crosstown Traffic/Gypsy Eyes Track 604 029 (4.69)

Right:
Electric Ladyland double
album.

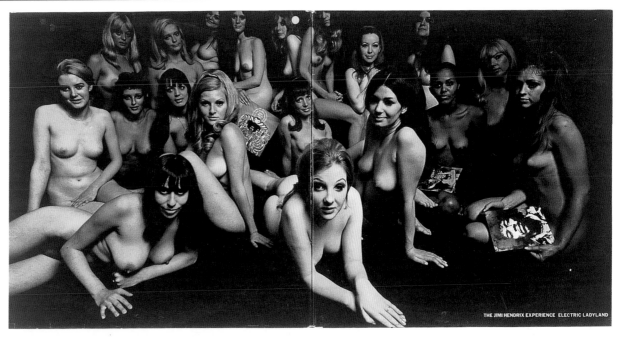

ELECTRIC LADYLAND Track 613 009 (10.68)
US Reprise 2RS 6307

SIDE 1   And The Gods Made Love; Electric Ladyland;
          Crosstown Traffic; Voodoo Chile.
SIDE 2   Little Miss Strange; Long Hot Summer Night; Come On;
          Gypsy Eyes; Burning Of The Midnight Lamp.
SIDE 3   Rainy Day Dream Away; 1983 (A Merman I Should
          Turn To Be); Moon Turn The Tides . . . Gently, Gently
          Away.
SIDE 4   Still Raining Still Dreaming; House Burning Down; All
          Along The Watchtower; Voodoo Chile (Slight Return).

GUEST MUSICIANS: 'Rainy Day Dream Away' and 'Still Raining
          . . .' – Mike Finnegan, organ; Freddie
          Smith, horn; Larry Faucette, congas; Buddy
          Miles, drums.
          '1983' – Chris Wood, flute.
          'Voodoo Chile' – Stevie Winwood, organ;
          Jack Casady, bass.
          'Long Hot Summer Night' – Al Kooper,
          piano.

          All Titles by Jimi Hendrix except 'Little
          Miss Strange' by Noel Redding; 'Come On'
          by Earl King; 'All Along The Watchtower'
          by Bob Dylan.
          Produced by Jimi Hendrix.

Left:
Jimi in the studio, 1968.

Jimi and Mitch at the Record Plant working on 'Electric Ladyland'. 1968.

THE TOUR, OR AT LEAST THE FIRST HALF OF it, wound down at the beginning of April. The most notable gig in the last few days was the Symphony Hall, Newark, New Jersey, the night after the assassination of Martin Luther King on April 5. This was a really frightening occasion with the National Guard out and tanks on street corners. In the end the band played the first show, the second being cancelled – probably a wise move under the circumstances.

The following month or so was devoted to recording their third album, 'Electric Ladyland'. Despite the conditions under which it was recorded, which Mitch describes, the result set new standards for rock recordings, featuring a breathtaking range of material, from the straight rock of 'All Along The Watchtower' to the inspired jamming of 'Voodoo Chile' and Jimi's much-vaunted 'sound painting', '1983 (A Merman I Should Turn To Be)'. The bulk of the recording was done in April and May in New York, but some pieces were started earlier than that in London.

After we finished 'Axis' and before we left for the second US tour, some recording was done at Olympic in London, including the original four-track versions of 'Crosstown Traffic' and Bob Dylan's 'All Along The Watchtower' which were transferred to sixteen-track in New York later on. We also did 'Tax Free', which is probably the version that came out on one of those posthumous albums. That cropped up live several times over the years, and I hope Hansson and Carlsson have got some royalties for it. Unlikely, but who knows?

I've also seen something listed from that period at Olympic called 'Mushy Name'. God knows what that was, could be one of mine. There are a couple of things of mine that have never surfaced, including a vocal, which hopefully will never see the light of day.

The bulk of the recording from then on took place at the Record Plant, in New York. We went there because Gary Kellegran, who

Jimi in the Record Plant, 1968.

*Jimi at the Fillmore
East, May 1968.*

we'd worked with at Mayfair, had raised the money with a partner and managed to start the Record Plant. I guess we started there, specifically to work on 'Electric Ladyland' around the middle of April 1968 after the first half of the tour with The Soft Machine had finished.

We block-booked the studio through the night. The usual thing was that late in the evening we'd go down to the Scene to play and hang out and then go round to the studio, which was only a couple of blocks away. Huge amounts of money were spent, not just on studio time, but in stupid things like having limos on call the whole time. We'd have them waiting around outside the Scene for hours, to take us and all our friends and anything that moved, two blocks down the street.

The security at the Record Plant wasn't terribly good and Hendrix would turn up with endless streams of people, so to get any kind of work done was really difficult. Looking back it was amazing that the album was finished. In the end the bulk of it got done in about a month, although at the time it seemed to take forever. Not just the album tracks, there were loads of out-takes that are now surfacing as well.

Mostly I did enjoy working on it, things like 'Voodoo Chile', with Jack Casady on bass plus Stevie Winwood and Chris Wood, were great. People like to make out that we were all playing together in the Scene and it was, 'Hey, let's take this down to the studio.' It wasn't really like that. Nice story though.

It was a good studio to work in, different from Olympic which was a big cathedral-like space. The Record Plant was much smaller, but had an excellent sound. It also had a twelve-track and later sixteen-track facility, as against just four at Olympic, which gave Jimi much more space to work in. Things did get chaotic though and Chas got pissed off with the way things were going, partly with Jimi's attitude, partly with Mike Jeffery – he just didn't need the aggravation.

Jimi wanted more freedom in the studio and more control, which was fine, but someone should have had more overall control. As much as there were good things that came out of the 'Electric Ladyland' sessions there was far too much wasted time and energy. It wasn't that I didn't enjoy all the partying; I did, but it was no way to work.

Jimi in the studio on keyboards, New York, 1968.

By that time the pressure was off us to record hit singles, which was great. The market had changed and you could become, to all intents and purposes, an album band, which is what we'd always wanted. For us, recording was a completely separate thing from playing live and I'm very proud of the fact that we were able to deliver the goods on both fronts in very different ways.

Jimi's self-indulgence of re-recording endless basic takes, which was what got Chas, would have been OK today – or would have at least cost less. With today's equipment he could have worked on his own much more and he could have used whatever bits of whatever takes he wanted. Back then, if you didn't like part of a take you'd have to go on to the next one. Chas couldn't handle it and neither could Noel.

Noel would just say, 'Fuck it', and leave

Mitch at the Paris Olympia, January 1968.

the studio, but then he'd done that at Olympic. Noel also reacted badly to the idea of guest musicians, whereas we loved it. It was one of the finest things in life – I mean, how lucky can you be – to work with all those people, in and out of the studio.

Along with this was Jimi's realization that he'd made it in America and he wanted to live permanently in New York. This, of course, was completely alien to Chas and Noel and even to me at that stage. It took me about a year to realize how important New York had become for me. I knew I was having fun there, but I used to knock the place. Then I suddenly realized how much work I was able to do there – I could lift up the phone and go and play with practically anyone I wanted. I realized how much I owed the place. But I can understand Noel and Chas's attitude.

Jimi at the Paris Olympia, January 1968.

Jimi and Mitch taking a few hours break in Miami, May 1968.

The other thing that did upset me, as well as Noel, was that we discovered Jimi was going out and buying guitars, drums for friends, in fact loads of stuff for virtually anybody and then charging them to the band's account. All in all I'm not surprised that Chas finally quit and went home.

One of the problems with the Electric Ladyland period was that we hardly played live while we were recording it. Consequently when we did play live we weren't as sharp as we might have been. I remember we did do

the Fillmore East during that time (May 5), with Sly And The Family Stone and, boy, were they hot. I felt comfortable playing, but the lack of playing gigs did make it that much tougher for all of us. Jimi and I really liked Sly And The Family Stone; Noel didn't, but then he didn't like James Brown either.

Just after that we were booked to do some gigs in England and for virtually the first time Jimi pulled a moody and refused to leave New York, just for a couple of days. In the past, if we were booked, we did the gig,

Jimi at the Miami Pop Festival, May 1968.

although all of us had complained about some of the itineraries, especially on that second American tour.

The other gig around that time was the Miami Pop Festival (May 18). It was suggested we should do it as it was a prestigious gig. There had never been much of a rock situation in Florida, but someone obviously thought it would be a good idea. It was held at Gulfstream Park Race Course and was organized by this guy Marshall Brevitz, who apparently handed over wads of cash to Mike Jeffery, which we never saw. Anyway, we were booked for two shows, Saturday afternoon and evening.

We'd been out partying the night before, got to bed about seven, so by the afternoon show, we were pretty tired. Anyway this guy comes along and says, 'Hey guys, I've got a little something here to perk you up,' and through foolishness, Hendrix and I accepted. We thought it was some sort of speed or amphetamine to give us some extra energy but it turned out to be some sort of hallucinogenic. We never did find out exactly what it was, except that it was a big mistake. We got on stage and on the second number I looked up and saw the guy who gave us the powder in a lighting tower about twenty-five feet above the stage.

Suddenly I was on the same level as him, looking down at this empty shell playing the drums. Obviously the powder wasn't what we thought! I looked across and there's Jimi up there with me and we kind of look at each other and nod, kind of, 'Gig going OK so far?' I have no idea if it was fact or fiction, it was straight out of the *Twilight Zone*.

It was really the first time we'd gone through that situation, 'cos we'd been spiked and badly at that. We looked down and saw Noel, who definitely knew that something strange was going on. He looked totally bewildered. Musically it was fine and we did our set and were looking forward to the second show at 7.30, or something like that.

Suddenly one of those huge thunderstorms appeared, the sort you only get down there and the second show was cancelled – rain stopped play. We'd all psyched ourselves up to play, so several of the people on the bill, including us, went off to find somewhere else. We ended up in this little hotel on the beach called Castaways with, among other people, Frank Zappa and Arthur Brown singing.

ALTHOUGH JIMI PULLED OUT OF A COUPLE OF English shows during the recording of 'Electric Ladyland', the band did come back to Europe for a few weeks after the Miami washout. Although they played several gigs, the whole trip had the air of a much needed holiday, which in the end it became.

I think we'd more or less finished the basic 'Electric Ladyland' recordings when we made our first trip to Italy. The first night in Milan was a strange kind of disco affair, but no big deal – a gig. Rome was very pleasant. I remember that Hendrix nearly got arrested. We had been to the Coliseum and were caught by the police at dawn with several young ladies.

'What are you doing?'

'What do you think we're doing!'

The last gig was in a modern sports stadium in Bologna, where we did an afternoon show. There was a riot, which I think had already started when we arrived – overpriced tickets or something, you never really found out about these things. We did our set, but had to leave pretty damn quickly. Very pleasant four days, more of a holiday really. Jimi and I really loved Italy.

A few days later we did this thing called the Beat Monster Concert in Zurich, with

LEFT:
Poster for the Woburn Abbey Music Festival, July 1968.

RIGHT:
Jimi with friends from left to right Carl Wayne, Steve Winwood, John Mayall, and Eric Burdon.

what was almost a package-tour-size line-up including The Move and Traffic. It took place in an indoor cycle-racing track, which was heavily greased. John Mayall went on first. He had a big band at the time and he didn't go down at all well and the kids started throwing these folding chairs.

We thought, 'Christ, what are they going to be doing by the time we get on!' When the riot started the police got the batons out and started beating the kids. The kids obviously thought, 'Enough of this,' and about eight of them linked arms across the steeply banked and heavily greased cycle track, from top to bottom. They started pulling police up the slope and because it was so slippery they couldn't do anything about it. They pulled the police up to the top, let them go and watched them go splat down at the bottom.

We went down fine as it turned out, I certainly had a good play.

Shortly after the Zurich thing, we managed a few days off in Majorca, where Mike Jeffery had always maintained an

San Francisco jam session (l to r) Eric Burdon, Mitch, Jimi, Jack Casady and Buddy Miles, 1968.

apartment. He'd just opened a club called Sgt. Pepper's, financed by us and his other acts, though we didn't know it at the time. Very nice. I think we played on the opening night, nothing serious, Noel playing guitar, Jimi on bass, that sort of thing.

Jimi was a fine bass player, one of the best, very Motown-style. He was a very busy bass player, which in retrospect was so good for me to have played behind as it stopped me overplaying, which I did do particularly on several of the album tracks. Maybe that was the source of the friction between Noel and Hendrix, Noel being a frustrated guitarist and Jimi knowing exactly what he wanted from the bass.

'All Along The Watchtower' is a classic example of Hendrix's bass-playing. Even being left-handed he had no problem picking up a right-handed bass – he just had the touch. I think Noel had got pissed off and was across the road in the pub – but the track didn't suffer.

On the same European trip we did do a couple of gigs in England. We guested on the *Dusty Springfield TV Show*, which wasn't bad. Jimi and Dusty duetted on 'Mockingbird', the only time we ever did the song. The other thing was the Woburn Abbey Pop Festival.

THE SECOND HALF OF THE SOFT MACHINE TOUR started at the end of July 1968 and ground on for another couple of months. One memorable gig was at the natural amphitheatre at Red Rocks, near Denver at the beginning of September. An absolutely beautiful and amazing place and by all accounts a wonderful gig. Around that time it was decided that the band should spend some time based in Los Angeles at

a rented house in Benedict Canyon.

LA was and remains a very different place from New York, the other city where the band spent a lot of time. The obvious difference is the geography, LA being a huge, sprawling mass of suburban canyons and beach towns. This meant that in terms of the music and related social scene, the city lacked any real equivalent of the Greenwich Village or Haight-Ashbury communities, although Sunset Strip provided some kind of focus for the kids. Throughout the mid-Sixties the Strip was home to several clubs like the Whiskey A Go-Go and Pandora's Box and hang-outs like Ben Franklin's, but it was always more nebulous in comparison with New York or San Francisco.

It was also a town of affluence and style. Even the street kids paid more attention to 'fashion' than elsewhere — there was little of the thrift-store ethic in LA. In fact the real scene was among the young movie-makers, actors and successful musicians who lived in secluded residences in the hills. Despite the existence of some very fine bands in LA, like Love, Kaleidoscope and Clear Light, the city's music was branded, particularly by San Franciscans, as 'plastic'. Groups like The Byrds, The Doors and even Buffalo Springfield (with Neil Young and Steve Stills) were held up as bands cynically exploiting the new scene.

The Experience were probably unaware of this and quite rightly would have been unmoved by it if they'd known. LA was a good place to be based and an excellent place to both work and relax. Even so, life in the canyon could get a little weird at times.

The house came with staff and security dogs and we'd only been there about a week, when the dogs got stolen. They were found wandering on Sunset Boulevard, doped out of their minds – that really pissed me off. The burglars had also nicked guitars and clothes and stuff, this being the first time that we had seen any kind of money at all, with which to buy anything. Hendrix had the Stingray he'd ordered earlier; this led to us realise later how bad his eyesight was – he should not have been driving.

One Saturday night we went to see Cream and we had a party back at the house. The party didn't break up until five and at about seven when I'd just got off to sleep, I heard Jimi's voice, 'Guess what, I've just crashed my car.' I thought I was dreaming and went back to sleep.

Several hours later I discovered that it was true. How the hell he survived, I've no idea. He'd completely demolished the car. Luckily he'd turned right and gone into some rocks. If he'd gone left he'd have gone straight over the edge of the canyon, a 300 foot drop.

There were often problems at the house. Firstly some of the Manson Family appeared in our absence, trying to see us. Then all these loonies would start climbing over the gates and really freak the staff out. We'd get back and find them there and Gerry Stickells would have to throw them out.

We were trying to keep a low profile in

terms of the public and it was a large enough house for us all to have privacy. Several of us lived there, including Robert Wyatt of Soft Machine, who lived downstairs by the games room. It was actually a lovely house. We began to hear various stories, that certain sections of the authorities, for whatever reason, were not pleased about our popularity and whatever they thought we stood for. Word reached us that we should watch our step.

One day – Hendrix was away at the time – I got a call from Noel. It was late on a Friday night and I was down at the Whiskey A Go-Go. Noel was saying, 'I think you better get up here right now. There are three blokes here. I don't know if we're talking police or Family or what.'

I got the security guy to drive back with me. We crept in through the kitchen door and as soon as I walked into the living room, I saw the 'shoes'. I realized that we were talking serious business. They said, 'We've been watching the house and we know what's going on and we're gonna bust your asses.' They had a drink and promptly left – 'Thanks for telling us chaps.' Noel and I got the shakes for about twenty minutes.

We'd found out that the previous resident had been Cary Grant, who admitted in a magazine that he'd taken acid. So who knew what was still on the premises. We kept a pretty clean, well-run house, I mean it wasn't a hippie palace or anything, but we were still worried. So that night we went through the entire house and it was OK, we didn't find anything. It was a scare tactic basically and in fact they left us alone, at least on the West Coast.

A lot of strange sessions came out of that period at TTG Studios, in LA – like a session with Graham Bond – most of which have never been released. We actually worked very hard while we lived there, it wasn't all hanging out. We did the first tryout of 'Izabella' there and 'Look Over Yonder' came out on 'Rainbow Bridge.' Jimi and I had a play with Carole Kaye, the bass player who did a lot of sessions for Motown, after they moved to LA. She was brilliant, scared

ABOVE: Final adjustments before show.

the shit out of me. Basically, though, the sessions at TTG were a lot of jamming in the studio with various people, most of which are hard to pin down as they never had titles.

Marshall Brevitz who'd done the Miami Pop Festival opened a club in LA at that time called 'The Experience'. Thank you, Marshall. It became a home from home for us. Sort of like a West Coast Scene club. I remember seeing Jimmy Page playing with The Bonzo Dog Band there, one night. Marshall was actually murdered a couple of years ago, presumably owing money to the wrong people.

Jimi at the Hollywood Bowl, September 1968.

We began to hear various stories, that certain sections of the authorities, for whatever reason, were not pleased about our popularity and whatever they thought we stood for. Word reached us that we should watch our step.

AT THE END OF THEIR BENEDICT CANYON sojourn the band did another set of gigs for Bill Graham in San Francisco. This was their third and, as it turned out, last visit to the city (although they did play across the Bay in Berkeley on the last tour). The second visit had been back at the start of the second US tour, in February (1–4) when they had been supported by John Mayall's Bluesbreakers and Albert King. By that time Graham had started using the much larger Winterland building for bigger gigs or dividing the nights up between the Fillmore and Winterland. For the February gigs, two had been in the old building and two in Winterland. In June 1968, Graham moved the Fillmore to more spacious premises at Market and Van Ness Streets across town, but despite this, when The Experience came to town in October (10–12) they were, not surprisingly, deemed worthy of a full complement of gigs at Winterland.

The October Winterland gigs have passed into legend as being among the band's finest perform-

gave each of us these beautiful antique pocket watches. I thought I'd lost mine, but luckily I found it quite recently – my father had been looking after it for twenty years. Noel tells me that Jimi lost his within two days; Noel then gave him his, which he managed to lose as well.

We always tried to do something special at the Winterland or Fillmore. On these gigs we probably jammed more and had lots of guests up like Jack Casady and Virgil Gonsalves and Herbie Rich, from Buddy Miles' band. Usually, when we worked for Graham we went next door after the proper gig to this masonic hall place, for some after-hours playing, which is perhaps where the stories of five-hour jams comes from.

We moved back to New York after the Benedict Canyon period and did a few East Coast gigs, including the Philharmonic Hall in New York. We'd always wanted to play Carnegie Hall, but they wouldn't have us. In

Poster for Winterland concerts in San Francisco, October 1968.

> *People always say that Bill Graham was a hard-arsed promoter, but he was always good to us and usually gave us a bonus. I think it was after these gigs that he gave each of us these beautiful antique pocket watches.*

ances, although tales of five-hour jams are somewhat far-fetched. There is no doubt, as the recorded evidence shows, that the band really stretched out on those gigs, one version of 'Are You Experienced' being over twenty minutes long. They also had frequent guests up to play with them. Some of the music from those nights has been released as a double album set, but good though the music is, only the shorter, more standard length tracks were selected.

We did the Winterland again in October of 1968, for three nights, with Buddy Miles' Express opening. People always say that Bill Graham was a hard-arsed promoter, but he was always good to us and usually gave us a bonus. I think it was after these gigs that he

lieu of that we were offered the Philharmonic, which was great. Lovely hall, very prestigious, no rock band had ever played there.

Only one problem, a member of the band had to play in a symphonic context. Jimi and Noel flatly refused, so I thought OK, what the hell, *I'll* do it. Would I mind having tea with Leonard Bernstein? Which I did; charming chap. He suggested that I might like to play percussion with The New York Brass Ensemble.

It was fine, I went on with them, with a collar and tie on and did some Bach and a little Mozart after which The Experience played. It was a great gig and the whole thing was filmed and I'd love to see it.

B
Y THE END OF 1968 THERE DID SEEM TO BE
a lack of direction in the band. Jimi was
spending more and more time in New
York and obviously wanted to base himself
there. There was no real friction, except over the
self-indulgence in the studio, but there was a
brief falling-out to the extent that Hendrix wrote
an apology to Noel and Mitch, although Mitch
can't remember exactly what the argument was
about. Noel and Mitch did come back to
England, but it was just a Christmas break as far
as Mitch and Jimi were concerned – not the
break-up the press were predicting.

*Recording a radio
session for the BBC.*

LEFT:
*Turning up the feedback; just one of the
special effects Jimi pioneered.*

Winterland Arena, San Francisco 10–12.10.68

10.10 First Show: Are You Experienced; Voodoo Chile; Red House; Foxy Lady; Like A Rolling Stone; Star Spangled Banner; Purple Haze.
Note: Several stereo recordings were made at the soundboard but the introductions are missing and the mixing is of variable quality.
10.10 Second Show: Tax Free; Lover Man; Sunshine Of Your Love; Hear My Train A Comin'; Killing Floor; Hey Joe; Star Spangled Banner; Purple Haze.
Note: Jack Casady of Jefferson Airplane replaced Noel Redding on 'Killing Floor' and 'Hey Joe' and again there were soundboard stereo recordings done.
11.10 First Show: Are You Experienced/Jam; Voodoo Chile; Red House; Foxy Lady; Star Spangled Banner; Purple Haze.
Note: Virgil Gonsales plays flute on 'Are You Experienced'. Both soundboard stereo recording and a recording done by someone in the audience exist.
11.10 Second Show: Tax Free; Spanish Castle Magic; Like A Rolling Stone; Lover Man; Hey Joe; Fire; Foxy Lady; (plus – possibly – Purple Haze).
Note: There was an audience recording done of at least three songs 'Fire', 'Hey Joe', and 'Foxy Lady', possibly more. There was the usual soundboard stereo recordings. Herbie Rich plays organ on everything except 'Tax Free', 'Spanish Castle Magic', and 'Purple Haze'.
12.10 First Show: Fire; Lover Man; Like A Rolling Stone; Foxy Lady; Jam/Tax Free; Hey Joe; Purple Haze; Wild Thing.
Note: The soundboard recording done for the first show was not mixed very well. There was an audience recording done which seems to have disappeared completely.
12.10 Second Show: Foxy Lady; Manic Depression; Sunshine Of Your Love; Little Wing; Spanish Castle Magic; Red House; Voodoo Chile; Star Spangled Banner; Purple Haze.
Note: Again this was recorded at the soundboard and supposedly by someone in the audience as well – but this has never surfaced at all.

Jimi at the Los Angeles recording studio, T.T.G. 1968.

Jimi working at T.T.G.

CASTLES MADE
of
SAND

RUMOURS OF AN IMMINENT SPLIT IN THE BAND, were further fuelled by the announcement that Noel had formed his own band, Fat Mattress. But for Mitch and Jimi, at least, the idea of outside activities was no great news. It was really only an extension of playing with other people as they had often done at The Scene and elsewhere. At the end of the day they'd always come back and play together, regardless of whoever else they'd been playing with in the meantime.

In the event the rumours were quashed, if only temporarily, by the announcement of a New Year European tour, followed by a series of US dates. If Noel made any stipulations, the only apparent one was that Fat Mattress opened the shows. Before the tour started, however, they had one extra date in England, *The Lulu Show* on BBC television.

The first thing we did prior to the New Year European tour was *The Lulu Show*, which has since passed into legend. The main thing to say about that is that as soon as we arrived, they said, as they had done with *The Dusty Springfield Show*, 'What about a duet, gotta do a duet with Lulu.' At the rehearsal Hendrix said, 'No problem, we'll do the duet on the show, we'll deal with it then.' I think she was supposed to do 'Hey Joe' or something.

Before the show itself comes the story of the lost 'substance'. We were hanging around in the dressing-room waiting to go on getting bored, as you always do on these occasions, and Noel decided to roll a joint, not the best idea considering where we were. Unfortunately he dropped the stuff down the sink. Panic, absolute panic. What do we do? I decide, no problem, pick up the phone and call Maintenance.

The guy arrives and we tell him we've lost a ring, so he proceeds to take the entire sink

BELOW:
The Jimi Hendrix Experience at the BBC-TV studios to film 'The Lulu Show', January 4th 1969.

124

LEFT:
Jimi relaxing in a London pub. January 1969.

BELOW:
The Experience waiting to go on 'The Lulu Show' BBC-TV. January 1969.

ABOVE LEFT:
German poster for the
J.H.E., January 1969.

ABOVE:
European Tour – 1969.

HAROLD DAVISON PRESENTS
AN EVENING WITH

Jimi Hendrix Experience

THE SOFT MACHINE
MASON, CAPALDI
WOOD & FROG
LONDON · ROYAL ALBERT HALL
TUESDAY, 18 FEB., at 7.30 p.m.
TICKETS: 3/6, 7/6, 10/6, 13/6, 16/6, 21/-
Available from ROYAL ALBERT HALL BOX
OFFICE (589 8212) and HAROLD DAVISON
LTD., REGENT HOUSE, 235-241 REGENT
STREET, LONDON, W.1

*Please send stamped addressed envelope with
postal applications*

*H endrix goes into his thing about Cream and off we go into,
'Sunshine Of Your Love'. It seemed to go down quite well. We went
back to the dressing room, quick change and then up to the BBC
Club for a drink. We walk in there and someone said the inevitable,
'You will never work for the BBC again!' The arm was pointing at
the door. Lulu, bless her heart didn't mind at all.*

Jimi and fans backstage. Frankfurt 1969.

apart. As soon as he got close to the relevant pipe, we're going, 'Don't worry, it's all right. We'll get it back.'

He, of course is saying, 'No, no, lads, it's all right, it's me job.' Noel is literally having to force him out of the way, but we eventually got it.

Anyway, come the show, we played our number and then at the end of the show Lulu starts to walk across to camera, expecting naturally, to do the duet, but Hendrix goes into his thing about Cream and off we go into, 'Sunshine Of Your Love'. It seemed to go down quite well.

We went back to the dressing-room, quick change and then up to the BBC Club for a drink. We walk in there and someone said the inevitable, 'You will never work for the BBC again!' The arm was pointing at the door.

Lulu, bless her heart, didn't mind at all. One thing to make clear about it is that it was a spontaneous thing, at least as far as I was concerned. Hendrix may have planned it from the afternoon, who knows? However, it's frequently reported that it was the only time we played it. In fact we'd been doing it for months and continued to do it for some time to come, on and off.

Also, of course, Cream had announced their retirement back in August 1968 or something – we certainly hadn't just received the news. I think Jimi was basically wishing them luck for whatever each of them was going to do. Either way, I'm really proud that we did it and I'm glad Hendrix had the balls to carry it through – it's really what live TV is about. You can actually see a look of surprise on my face and my drumming on it does leave something to be desired, but what the hell.

Anyway, shortly after *The Lulu Show* we started the European tour. This time – and this was another scatterbrained Mike Jeffery scheme – we would film the whole tour. Good idea, but he got these 'film makers' Gold and Goldstein, who'd already filmed the Philharmonic gig, to do it. They came along with us, filmed everything in sight, but what happened to the film, we don't really know. Bits have turned up on MTV, bits have been sold off and various divorce settlements have meant that ex-wives have bits. But, all in all, they must still have some damned good footage, but we've never seen it.

The tour itself was fine. The usual well-organized German gigs, where we were well taken care of. Another road tour, drive, get to the gig, sound-check, hotel. It would have been good, especially by this stage, to have had time off between the gigs – if only to get the equipment set up properly in each place.

We were generally down to one show per night, which was much better and it meant we could stretch out. Sound-checks were playing a more prominent part too but we were still using primarily the house PA. As in Vienna, for instance, a beautiful concert hall, but not made for rock 'n' roll.

On the whole we enjoyed the tour, we all liked being on the road, but it was a bit of a grind. We were still largely going back to places we'd done before, even if the halls were a bit larger and more prestigious.

The tour ended with two shows at the Royal Albert Hall in London, in February, on successive Mondays. Both sold out, but the first was appalling. One of those gigs where you wished you could go back the next night to make up for it, but you had to wait a week. I don't know what it was, it just didn't feel good. It was one of those gigs when your parents are there, it's the big event, but funnily enough most people enjoyed it.

The stage setting was odd on the first show, it was like being in the round and the house lights were on for the first one, which didn't help the atmosphere. The sound used to bounce around all over the place too. It's better now, but then it was terrible, again especially on the first show.

Anyway we changed the setting for the second show and it felt much better. I seem to remember it was on that one that Dave Mason and Chris Wood came up and joined us at the end for a jam. Yeah, good show. Ironically, I think they only filmed the first show, although I'm told there is a sound recording of the second, fortunately.

WHEN THE TOUR FINISHED THE BAND returned to the States. With two months off before the next US dates, Hendrix took advantage of the situation by spending as much time as possible in the studio. A few sessions took place with Mitch and Noel, the last ever by The Experience, but they were uniformly unproductive. Mostly it was a period of Jimi's trying out various studios, sometimes only for a few hours, usually with Mitch. It was basically more jamming, with various 'guest' musicians, like John McLaughlin, Dave Holland and Larry

Young – very much a jazz-influenced period.

Some of the sessions were arranged by jazz producer Alan Douglas, whose wife, Stella, also made clothes for Jimi and Mitch. In theory the 'new' direction was a good one for Hendrix, but in Mitch's estimation, Douglas didn't work out as a producer for Jimi and none of the 'jazz' sessions appeared during Hendrix's lifetime and only bits and pieces have cropped up since.

We started the last tour with Noel in Raleigh, North Carolina, on April 11. We'd definitely been moved up to bigger venues by this stage, some we'd done before, but the whole tour now was played in vast arenas. Yet again the sound in most of them was awful. We all preferred the smaller halls we had been doing, where there was at least some chance of the audience hearing something, although they still seemed to enjoy it. However, the majority also seemed to want more equipment smashing and guitar burnings – it was all starting to wear a little thin, especially for Hendrix.

The tour really was the same old stuff, right down to the same room-service menu you'd seen the night before in a different city. Here we were, doing the same old places and an anger or at least an annoyance started creeping in that we still hadn't played in Japan or Australia or even South America. Boredom was setting in too and the only thing you can do to relieve it, in terms of work, is the recording studio. The problem, was that as a band we needed that contact with a live audience.

We were still enjoying the occasional gig, but it *was* only the occasional one. Noel was getting more involved with his own band, Fat Mattress. He had insisted they open for us in Europe and they were doing so on this tour as well. I always thought that was strange, him doing that and Jimi resented it. Fat Mattress were just OK, but essentially a pretty lightweight band. Hendrix used to call them Thin Pillow. Incredible as it may seem after all Noel's hustling for Fat Mattress, they bounced him out a short time later, gratitude, eh?

Part of the problem, too, was that

Jimi at the San Jose Pop Festival, May 1969.

San Jose Pop Festival, May 1969.

Mitch in the studio, New York City 1968.

LEFT:
Chas Chandler and Jimi at the Albert Hall, February 1969.

Royal Albert Hall, London 18.2.69

Tax Free; Fire; Hear My Train; Foxy Lady; Sunshine Of Your Love; Spanish Castle Magic; Star Spangled Banner; Purple Haze; Voodoo Chile.
Note: There was an audience recording of this show which has turned up on two bootleg L.Ps. A black and white film exists but it is not very good.

Royal Albert Hall, London 24.2.69

Lover Man; Stone Free; Hear My Train A Comin'; I Don't Live Today; Red House; Foxy Lady; Sunshine Of Your Love; Bleeding Heart; Little Wing; Voodoo Chile; Purple Haze; Star Spangled Banner; Room Full of Mirrors.
Note: There was a bootleg L.P. done at the *soundcheck*! The tracks included several takes of 'Hound Dog' as well as three or four Experience classics. There was the usual soundboard recording of the performance.

Hendrix was receiving very little direction from the management. He was one of those people who, even in the early days, took little notice of his accounts. He would turn up at the office or send a letter to the accountants – 'Oh, I want a few thousand dollars.'

Mike Jeffery was getting into mysticism at this point. We're talking about ostensibly a bright man here. We never knew much about his background, but there were always stories of supposed involvement with MI5 or the CIA, somewhere in his background. When he ran the Club A Go-Go in Newcastle, he definitely had connections with the Newcastle 'Family'. He could certainly take care of business, but a lot of juggling was going on. His attitude with Jimi was as long as he wanted a new car or clothes or equipment, fine, just give him some more money.

To be honest I can only remember a handful of gigs on that tour. None were that memorable. We did the LA Forum for a couple of nights at the end of April. We'd all been looking forward to playing it, ever since we'd been there for the Cream farewell concert, back in Benedict Canyon days. Anyway, the gigs were all right, and the sound, for once was tolerable.

I remember clearly what took place on the second night, a Saturday. We'd all left and the road crew were packing up and someone ran up and grabbed one of my tom-toms and ran off with it – and got out of the bloody hall! The drum was never seen again and the road crew didn't tell me, the idea being that they wouldn't until they'd found another one. We're talking custom Ludwig drums here – without the missing one to balance them, the others would fall over. They had to chase around and open up a couple of stores on the Sunday to find a replacement in time for the gig that night.

We moved on from the Forum and a couple of nights later on May 2 we were playing the Cobo Hall in Detroit. I don't know how it was passed, but we received a message, probably from New York. One of the road crew, I think it was Gerry, came to us and said, 'You're playing Toronto tomorrow and word has got out that you're going to be busted,' no more, no less. 'Have you got anything?'

In a word, no. If there had been anything, it would have been sent back to New York in the washing, or disposed of. None of us would have knowingly carried stuff over a border, with or without prior knowledge of a bust. I had a specially made leather suit with no pockets, nothing, no underwear for these occasions. When we got off the plane, it was straight into customs and a strip search.

> *The tour really was the same old stuff, right down to the same room service menu you'd seen the night before in a different city. Here we were, doing the same old places and an anger or at least an annoyance started creeping in that we still hadn't played Japan or Australia or even South America.*

There was a certain amount of humour involved, at least from my part, knowing there was going to be a reception committee, but it wasn't even that thorough. We were all fairly convinced that this went back to the Benedict Canyon incident, when they'd told us that they were out for us.

I got the search, including this Gladstone bag that Jack Casady had given me. They found a packet of those scented tissue things you mop your brow with and thought they were giant rolling papers. That was about it for me, but with Hendrix, they found powder . . . heroin, in his bag.

I have to say that Hendrix was never great at packing. Everyone would be ready to leave the hotel and Gerry would go to Jimi's room and everything would be strewn across the floor from the night before. That did get on people's nerves, no doubt about that, especially if we ended up missing a flight. But for this one, Toronto, knowing what was going to happen, Gerry and Jimi would have gone through every item of clothing before packing them in the case.

We had the problem, of course, of fans slipping stuff to you without you knowing, but again they would have found anything

LEFT:
Jimi at the Newport Pop Festival, Los Angeles, June 1969.

while packing. In terms of what they actually found, well, if it had been a different substance, then it might possibly have been Hendrix's, but he didn't like heroin. So to my mind he was definitely set up.

Contrary to what some people have said, Jimi was *never* a junkie – that is he was *never* addicted to any drug, particularly heroin, which he had tried once or twice but didn't like. Also there is no truth in the story that our management ever forced dope down Jimi's throat. Drugs were certainly consumed in those days by bands on the road many of the same drugs used by millions of housewives and businessmen. They did become a way of life. Even if you tried to avoid yourself some asshole would come along and spike your drink. It was very hard to get away from.

After he was busted and booked, we had a problem, of course; we had a concert to play that night. We went to the hotel and Hendrix was still out at the airport with the Mounties and it was several hours before they let him out on bail. We did the gig, but as far as I remember we were actually escorted on stage by Mounties. How the hell, we . . . he played that night I don't know. They were definitely lacking in any kind of humour.

It wasn't the first time we'd gone through strange situations in Canada. We'd had some good times as well. One time we met up with the Chieftains, they were staying in the same hotel in Montreal, an unlikely crowd to be with us, but a jolly time was had by all.

Another time – in Quebec – we heard of this great girl singer in town, called Joni Mitchell. Hendrix and I both had these portable Sony tape recorders, huge things, that we dragged round the world. So we went to this little folk club, after our gig, with Hendrix's tape machine. We were amazed, she was wonderful. So we taped the show and then went back to the hotel.

Turns out, not only is she staying in the same hotel, but she's on the same floor. So we went to his room, just the three of us, played the tape back, compared notes, that kind of thing. It's two in the morning, but we're keeping things low and we'd been there

about an hour and the manager comes up. He went fucking berserk, 'You can't have guests in your room.'

What! We couldn't believe it. We were all staying on the same floor, for God's sake.

So we said, 'We can't have any guests in *this* room, right?'

'Yes.'

So we moved everything into my room. We got chased out of there and went to Joni's. This went on all night. Unfortunately the tape recorder and the tape were stolen the next day, so end of story on that, but strange guy. Who knows what it was? Black man, white man and white girl, I don't know.

Some of the Canadian gigs had been really good, great audiences, but the hotels had always been a bit odd. So the Toronto bust didn't come as a big surprise, especially, as I say, as we felt the thing had been set up by the Americans, for whatever reason. The only other thing to add is that, when he went back for his trial, they apparently found some acid on Hendrix. So either he was having some kind of mischievous fun with them – which seems unlikely, even for Hendrix – or they were trying to pull something else. Either way that didn't go any further.

THE GIGS FOLLOWING THE TORONTO BUST undoubtedly suffered as a result and Mitch is sure that the tour became even more of a grind after that. At the beginning of June they played a couple of dates in Hawaii after which they got some genuine time off. It's worth mentioning if only because Hendrix took what was probably the only real holiday he ever had. He went to Morocco with Deering Howe and Brian Jones and apparently was treated extremely well. Mitch is convinced he should have done that sort of thing more often.

After Jimi returned, our next date (June 20) was the Newport Pop Festival, Devonshire Downs, outside LA. God, what a tricky gig. It was the first gig, I think, where we were apparently being paid giant wads of cash. One gig, 45 minutes and the guarantee was well over a hundred grand. We knew this

Jimi Hendrix 'Experience' by Nona Hatay.

Jimi at Madison Square Garden, New York City, May 1969.

Jimi performing, spring 1969.

and it was obviously on our minds – not that it was obscene, just a bit odd.

I remember the gig, we got there about nine o'clock, got on about eleven, having spent a couple of hours in the caravan with an even greater than usual number of hangers-on. I don't know, but I think someone spiked Jimi or maybe he'd taken something of his own and then someone had spiked him on top of that. It was a disaster. I kept thinking, this is weird – all this money. It was almost like, how much per minute am

I getting? So that, plus Hendrix's state, added up to a terrible performance. Absolutely awful. We were devastated, it was one of the worst gigs we ever played.

On the drive back to LA, Jimi decided to go back, bless his heart, to play again. Not for any money or anything, just because he felt he wanted to make up for it. I didn't, not sure why, I just didn't want to visit the site again. Anyway Jimi went back on the Sunday and jammed with various people including Buddy Miles. He did the right thing as a musician, I wish I'd done it as well.

The other aspect of this is that our first gig in the States, Monterey, had been a festival, but it had been well organized and I'd enjoyed it. Newport Pop was probably the first of what was to become the norm for festivals, in that the whole thing was more like an army manoeuvre – the spirit had gone out of those kind of events.

B Y THIS TIME MITCH HAD PLAYED A COUPLE OF times with Billy Cox, at least in the studio. A good, solid, reliable bass player and a nice man. Noel was funny, always a constant source of musicians' gags and Jimi and Mitch certainly loved him for that and he was really good on stage, constantly strutting around. The

often discussed the possibilities of bringing in a horn section or whatever. Just thinking about what might work. If anything didn't work, fine – forget it. I really don't remember any animosity at the time, certainly not that afternoon.

Anyway, we did the gig, very good crowd. It seems, though, that the powers that be decided to use the place for a tear-gas experiment and an exercise in crowd control. They claimed that the crowd was getting out of control – absolute bull. OK, so a few people ran up to the front of the stage, but we're not talking serious lunacy here. Suddenly from the surrounding hills they let the tear-gas off and people started to panic.

We were virtually finishing our set when it

> *T*he other aspect of this is that our first gig in the States, Monterey, had been a festival, but it had been well organized and I'd enjoyed it. Newport Pop was probably the first of what was to become the norm for festivals, in that the whole thing was more like an army manoeuvre – the spirit had gone out of those kind of events.

bottom line, though, was that he was a frustrated guitar player and Mitch thinks that got a bit annoying for Jimi. When Jimi played with other bass players, like Jack Casady, who really loved playing bass, he noticed the difference.

Noel only played one more gig with us after Newport Pop, at the Mile High Stadium in Denver, at the end of June. I've read various things suggesting that Noel got very emotional about a reporter who said to him, 'What are you doing here? I thought you'd left?' That kind of deal. Maybe so, maybe not.

I do remember we attended a press conference in the afternoon and that was probably where Noel was approached essentially with the information that the band might be expanding. Well, this was no big news. I can't speak for Noel, but we'd

happened, and we were ushered off-stage through the tear-gas. Gerry Stickells suddenly, not for the first time, had a heavy situation to deal with. He found us a U-Haul Rent-A-Truck, one of those two-ton jobs, with aluminium sides and top. The band got into the back, this huge cavernous space. We only had to drive about a quarter of a mile back to the hotel, but suddenly we were very scared. To avoid the tear-gas, people started climbing on to the roof, which started to cave in, and we thought it was just a matter of moments before we were going to be crushed.

It took us nearly an hour to get back and we all linked arms and shook hands, feeling that if we were going to go, we'd go together. We really still felt like a band, absolutely no animosity. Either way Noel did fly back to England the next day and announced that he'd left the band.

LEFT:
Jerry Stickells and Jimi at London's Heathrow Airport, 1969.

ABOVE:
On stage in California, June 1969.

BELOW:
Posters for Devonshire Downs Pop Festival, Newport, California, 1969.

OPPOSITE PAGE:
'Entrance' by Nona Hatay 1969.

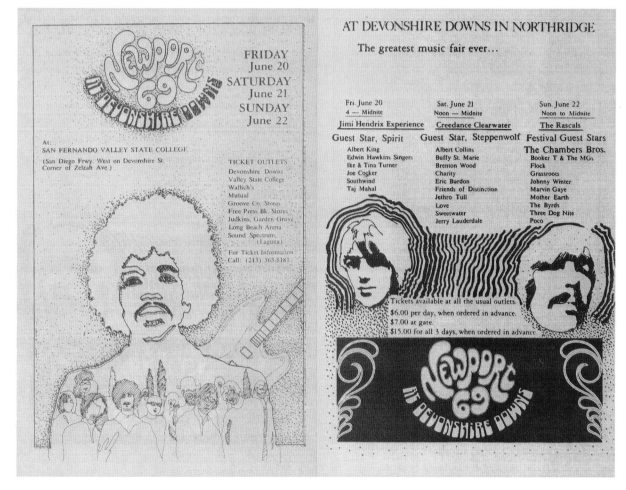

PEACE, MUD and TEARS

WHETHER THE TOUR WAS SUPPOSED TO END in Denver, no one can remember. In any event Denver was the last gig The Experience ever played. The period that followed was the most curious one of Hendrix's career, both professionally and privately. Between Denver and the start of his last tour in April 1970, leaving aside the perennial jamming, he played one festival, one street fair and two proper gigs.

I'm not sure if the tour was supposed to end in Denver, I assume so. I went back to New York for a few days and then went back to England, to the house I'd recently bought in Sussex. Later I flew back to do some sessions with Betty Davis, Miles's ex-wife and then returned to England once again. Jimi and I stayed in touch over the phone but we both really needed a break from the grind, what with the tour, problems with Noel and all the rest.

Then, at the beginning of August, I got a call to come up to his rural retreat near Woodstock. It's odd, because we're not talking about Mister Country-boy here. He loved looking at countryside from a moving car, but didn't ever want to stop off. The management had rented this obscene mansion, a really grim place and Jimi had installed Billy Cox and his lovely wife Brenda, and Larry Lee – a guitarist who Jimi had known for years. He was another guy who hadn't seen Jimi for ages and suddenly there is this whole other Hendrix to take in. Larry started putting a scarf round his head because he thought that's what hippies did – looked very strange. A nice man and more than adequate guitar player, but did Hendrix need a rhythm guitarist?

Also around were the two conga players, Jerry Valez – brother of Martha Valez the singer – and Juma Sultan, both good players in their own right but there's always a problem with two or more drummers or percussionists – either it works well or it gets competitive. It's all right having competition if you can count, if you can't, you're fucked. They couldn't count. The band was a shambles.

Apparently, they'd been working for about ten days when I got there, but you'd never have known. The band was grim and the house was grim. The only thing that had any humour was when Eric Barrett – who was there to look after Jimi and to try and get people out of bed to work – fired an air pistol at Mike Jeffery's approaching jeep and shattered the windscreen. That was the only funny moment – other than watching Hendrix attempt to ride a horse – definitely a sight to be reckoned with.

We were basically there, of course, because we were contracted to do the Woodstock Festival and I got the feeling several times during the rehearsals that Jimi realized it wasn't working and just wanted to get the gig over and start again. We rehearsed up at the house – which wasn't in Woodstock by the way, it was about 12 miles from any kind of civilization – for about a week or ten days. It was probably the only band I've ever been involved with that simply did not improve over that length of time.

Anyway, we were told that we were due on at the festival at 11 o'clock on the last night. The plan was to leave at about eight and go to the local airfield and get a helicopter in yet another army manoeuvre. By eight o'clock it was absolutely pissing down with rain – no

flights. We had to drive, which was a good long way. It's still pissing down and there was a hurricane blowing and, of course, the roads were jammed.

No one was in a great humour when we finally got there, especially as we stepped out of the car into about two feet of mud. The next thing was that the organizers told us that they're running about three hours late – wonderful. They also said that all the caravans were occupied, so we sort of shuffled on stage – I remember seeing Crosby, Stills and Nash – in an attempt to get on somehow. That failed and in the end they pointed out this cottage we could shelter in – it was about three muddy fields away.

So we squelched over there and spent the rest of the night literally freezing in there. We're not talking fun here.

Jimi and Billy Cox, at the Hit Factory, New York City, 1969.

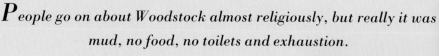

*P*eople go on about Woodstock almost religiously, but really it was mud, no food, no toilets and exhaustion.

Woodstock, New York 18.8.69

Message To Love; Lover Man; Hear My Train A Comin'; Spanish Castle Magic; Red House; Master Mind (blues jam); Foxy Lady; Beginnings; Izabella; Gypsy Woman (Larry Lee vocals); Fire; Voodoo Chile/Stepping Stone; Star Spangled Banner; Purple Haze; Villanova Junction Blues; Hey Joe.
Note: Larry Lee did the vocals on 'Master Mind' and on 'Gypsy Woman'. 'Jam Back at the House' listed as 'Beginnings' was actually written by Mitch Mitchell, not Hendrix as credited. Eddie Kramer did the soundboard recording and many different films or bits of film exist.

We had really been looking forward to playing, we knew it was going to be a *huge* event because talk had gone round the town for weeks while we were rehearsing.

But we were kept hanging around for hours, the mud and rain didn't help and the bands didn't really mix because if you were lucky enough to have a caravan you stayed there. Our enthusiasm dried up even more when it became apparent we were to get on-stage not Sunday night as planned but in the very early hours of Monday morning. We finally did get on about 6 a.m. Monday – Great.

Having waited up all night, the audience understandably seemed as groggy as we were – and it was horrible to see people packing up and leaving as we came on. Monday morning was back to the grind for a lot of people who'd come and it couldn't be helped.

It was so cold and damp at that time of the morning that none of our numbers really gelled – they just turned into long jams. There were a lot of stops and starts. We hadn't rehearsed or planned to do the 'Star Spangled Banner' at Woodstock but we often played it in America. It's become associated with Woodstock, and that's fine, but we did play it a lot. Sometimes I stuck in a few drums, sometimes not, but I did at Woodstock to keep my hands warm.

It was a real anti-climax. If only we could have gone on at night. There was no camaraderie when we came off – most of the others had gone. We had a long drive ahead of us and we just wanted to go home.

People go on about Woodstock almost religiously, but really it was mud, no food,

BELOW LEFT:
Unbelievably, Mitch 'round Woodstock time, August 1969.

BELOW:
Woodstock Rock Festival poster, August 1969.

no toilets and exhaustion.

After Woodstock I stayed over for quite some time in New York. I was in my hotel and Jimi still had his little apartment in the Village. We were checking out studios basically – the Hit Factory, the Record Plant bit – but that was winding down for us. No gigs, except for this Harlem Street Fair we did on September 5. It was a free gig on the back of a flat bed truck – a benefit as I remember, for a free clinic.

Jimi and I drove up through Central Park in the afternoon in his Stingray and parked on the street in Harlem. We'd only got about twenty feet from the car, when this group of like ten-year-old kids stole Jimi's guitar, which was on the back seat. It turned out the guys who were putting on the gig were the Allen Twins, also known as the Ghetto Fighters and old friends of Jimi's, and their family 'ran' the block. Apparently at that time various families 'ran' maybe two or three blocks of Harlem each.

Anyway the Allen Twins caught the kids and it was like 'Do you know whose guitar that is?'

'Yes' (giggle giggle).

'Well, give the guitar back.'

So we got it back, but I think if it hadn't been one of his favourites he would have probably said, 'Oh let 'em keep it.' I think he gave them money anyway.

We did the gig and it was like a big street fair. We played for an hour or something like that and it was fine except that a couple of eggs got thrown. Never knew if they were meant for me being the only whitey on stage, but they only hit some amplifiers in any case. The Allen Twins caught whoever did it and proceeded to beat the shit out of them. That was the only time I played in Harlem, but I had a great time whenever I went up there.

Jimi definitely wanted to stay in New York, but it was a bit of a difficult time for me. I'd bought the house in England and I'd hardly lived there. Jimi was all over the place, mentally and physically, but he did want to stay in New York, which was definitely encouraged by Mike Jeffery. Jimi had been going through this strange thing,

exemplified by the Woodstock band, of being almost fixated with being reunited with people from his past. Billy Cox, fine – good bass-player – but Larry Lee? I think he realized that he made a mistake, although he did do some recording with them in the month after Woodstock, but later things got trimmed down.

I went back to England, if only to spend some time in my house, but we stayed in contact by phone. He carried on working with Billy Cox and also Buddy Miles. Why not? It certainly seemed to make sense at the time.

BELOW:
Mitch, Jimi and band at Woodstock, August 1969.

RIGHT:
Billy Cox with Jimi. Billy was one of the nicest people you could ever meet, and an excellent bass player. He and his lovely wife, Brenda, were like family to Jimi.

Jimi had retained Billy Cox from the Woodstock line-up and in Mitch's absence – coupled with a general desire to play with other people – particularly those he'd known for a long time, Buddy Miles did indeed seem the obvious choice. They'd played together on and off for the previous year or so, mainly in the studio, but once or twice Buddy had played on stage with them, as at Winterland, and Jimi had jammed with Buddy's band, The Express. By September 1969 Jimi was rehearsing regularly with Buddy and Billy and it seems likely they appeared together, more or less unannounced at

J.H. EXP.

the Salvation Club, under the name Sky Church.

Following the rehearsals, Jimi took the others into the studio for nearly eight weeks of recording, starting in the beginning of November. Once again very little of the material surfaced during Hendrix's lifetime. As much as anything the studio time was used as a run-up to the gigs they had booked – New Year's Eve and the following night at the Fillmore East. The gigs were also being used to record a live album, to be given to record producer Ed Chalpin, who'd won a long-standing court case over a contract Hendrix had signed prior to leaving for Britain in 1966. They appeared under their new name of The Band Of Gypsys, but the gigs and the resulting album split fans – a lot like it, but just as many don't. Hendrix, too, seemed to have doubts almost straight away, as Mitch remembers.

I know that Jimi loved Buddy's drumming and singing, until he started working with him – certainly in terms of a performing band. There was no problem with Billy. Like Noel, you could tell Billy exactly what you wanted and he'd play it but Jimi didn't want that again, and luckily Billy always came up with his own ideas. I'm sure Jimi had the best motives, but to pull Billy out of the lounge clubs, where he'd been playing, to appear at Woodstock was not really fair. He had no time to prepare for it.

I was still in England at the end of the month (February 28) when The Band Of Gypsys did their second and final gig at Madison Square Garden. This was the one where something happened to Jimi, when he was spiked or whatever and walked off after a couple of numbers. Anyway, God knows what time it was for me, certainly the middle of the night, when Hendrix phoned. He was not happy generally, and certainly not happy with the direction of the band.

I had, in fact been playing during this period, with Jack Bruce and Larry Coryell. I knew The Band Of Gypsys thing was going to take place and, lo and behold, I got a call from Jack Bruce: 'Would I like to go and have a play with him and Larry?'

We went out as Jack Bruce And Friends

and did a short UK tour, followed by a gig at the Fillmore East, a couple of nights after Jimi's Madison Square Garden show. I was actually booked into a hotel, but I spent most of the following week staying with Jimi and Devon Wilson, Jimi's girlfriend, down in his apartment in the Village.

The pressure seemed to have eased off at that point. He knew he wasn't happy with The Band Of Gypsys, but he hadn't got anything else going on. It was a very comfortable time for the two of us. Whence the idea came I know not – maybe the management, maybe Jimi, maybe a bit of both – but the plan was: 'Why don't we re-form The Experience?'

I suspect the deal was that we would ultimately cover some of the places we'd not been to, like Japan and Australia; in fact rumour has it there were people selling tour jackets for Japan. Of course, we never got there in the end. I'm not sure how Noel got the call, but I don't think he'd even seen Jimi for six months. There was a meeting at the management office in New York with the three of us and then a lengthy interview with *Rolling Stone*, during which we announced the tour.

After the interview Jimi went back to his apartment and I went back to my hotel and within a few hours I'd got a call from him. 'Could we meet up?' Musically the conversation was over in a very short time. It came down to 'What do you think?' I knew that he meant Noel. It was very tricky. Jimi and I had great affection for Noel as a player and for his humour, but something didn't feel right.

Anyway I said, 'What do *you* think?' and he shook his head. I threw in Jack Casady as a possibility, but for some reason this wasn't possible. In the end it came out in Billy Cox's favour. There's no doubt he felt that he had to do the tour, because apart from anything else Electric Lady, his projected studio, was eating up huge sums of money. He was up to his arse in debt.

Anyway the unfortunate thing about Noel was that he wasn't told until he came back to America, expecting to rehearse for the tour.

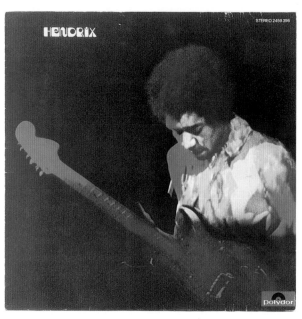

Band Of Gypsys Track 2406 002 (6.70) US Capitol STAO 472

Side 1 Who Knows; Machine Gun.
Side 2 Changes (a.k.a. 'Them Changes'); Power To Love (a.k.a. 'Power Of Soul') Message Of Love (a.k.a. Message To Love); We Gotta Live Together.

All tracks written by Jimi Hendrix except 'Changes' & 'We Gotta Live Together' which are by Buddy Miles.
Produced by 'Heaven Research'. Recorded live by Wally Heider.

*Left:
Current sleeve of Band of Gypsys album.*

Juma Sultan and Jerry Velez in the studio, 1969.

Jimi's girlfriend, Devon Wilson, summer 1969.

Basically no one had the balls to do it. As I understand it, Noel turned up at the airport, to be met by Bob Levine, who worked for Mike Jeffery, who told Noel, 'Hey, I've got a great drummer for you to play with.' I certainly didn't know that Noel hadn't been told, but I find it hard to believe that Hendrix, at least, hadn't done it.

If something bothered Jimi, he got on the phone and told you right away. I've heard that after he was given the news, Noel phoned my hotel and talked to someone who told him that I was in the studio working with Jimi and Billy, which is possible. We certainly did do some sessions before going on tour, but it was just bits and bobs again, a few of which have surfaced, like 'Earth Blues', which came out on 'Rainbow Bridge'. A few projects got put on hold as well, like the Gil Evans/Miles Davis thing. Alan Douglas was still around. Jimi certainly thought of him as a useful hustler, but as a producer, not first choice.

LEFT:
Billy Cox and Larry Lee in the studio, mid-1969.

ABOVE:
Mitch, July 1969.

THE TOUR WITH MITCH AND BILLY STARTED AT the LA Forum on April 25. They were to play 31 dates in just over three months, after which they were to have a month's break before going to Europe.

From the outset it became obvious to Mitch that the new band, although capable of producing good music, felt less exciting than the old one. Billy was a good, solid player, but he didn't do much except stand by his bass speakers and even Jimi seemed reluctant to produce a show. Whether he wanted it or not, however, it was still party-time back at Hendrix's hotel room.

For the Forum gig we were staying at Rodeo Drive again, at the hotel. I had a suite there; he had one with his own private elevator. Talk about hangers-on. I went up to see him once during the week we were there and stayed about two minutes. I thought, 'I don't

want anything to do with this.' He didn't want all these people around but he didn't know how to say no. The Forum gig was not very memorable. We went in, did the gig and left and it shouldn't have been that way.

A lot of the gigs were like that. I have to say that most of the gigs were unmemorable, the same old places, yet again. Billy Cox held things down very nicely, never any problem at all, a really stable person. But it was really starting to lose its rock 'n' roll flavour, even though on some gigs we did deliver the goods. If it had been something completely different, like the Miles Davis thing, that would have been great, but this was like the old band, but much less exciting.

Of course we did do Berkeley on this tour (May 30) during the riots. It was weird, not being a political band, that we were in the right – or perhaps the wrong – place at the

Jimi talks to writer Stephen Clackson, Londonderry Hotel, London 1969.

148

right time. We'd been through it in Chicago, looking out through the hotel window and seeing kids being beaten up really badly. It was really difficult to play that night. In Newark, New Jersey, there were tanks on the street and at Berkeley we arrived in the middle of mass confusion and demonstrations.

How this affected Hendrix, I'm not sure. A lot of things affected him afterwards and came out in some of the songs.

Jimi did look a bit rough around that time, you can see it in the Berkeley film. We were based in Rodeo Drive again, with all the hangers-on and he wasn't taking too much care of himself. We'd had a few days off before the gig, which can always do it to you. There is the possibility that he was pushing things to extremes.

After Berkeley it was a case of more stadium gigs and a couple more dreadful, army manoeuvre festivals at Atlanta and Randall's Island. By then they were weekend gigs, so things were easier, but the band were in the studio during most of the breaks, so the pressure was still on. By contrast the majority of the last gigs on the tour were, in their own way, memorable, the first of these being Mauii, Hawaii, which is preserved on film.

Mike Jeffery came up with the idea of putting together a recording complex cum homebase on Maui, based around geodesic domes designed by Buckminster Fuller. If it had happened it would have been a good idea. It didn't, of course, but land was found and plans were drawn up and an awful lot of money was spent that basically we didn't have.

Jeffery was taking increasingly large amounts of acid and getting further into mysticism. Somehow he met these two film makers who'd worked with Warhol, neither of whom could produce a piss-up in a brewery, and that's being kind.

Anyway, the gig itself, the one referred to as 'Rainbow Bridge' (July 30), took place between the Craters of The Sun and the Craters of The Moon, i.e. two extinct volcanoes. There was no publicity, they simply went round the island the day before with lorries and flower children and stuff and lo and behold the next day this huge number of people showed up. It surprised me as it was at least a three-mile hike up there.

We got there and there's the director asking the audience what star sign they are. They're going, 'OK, all the Aquarians over this side, thank you very much, Cancers, stage left, that'll do very nicely.'

They'd hired a basic, straight Hollywood film crew, who were just killing themselves laughing every time the director told the audience to link arms and chants om' or whatever. They'd lugged all this recording equipment up there, but because of the magnetic forces – this is for real . . . man – between the two volcanoes, a lot of the machines simply didn't work. When I came to re-mixing it, I discovered that only eight out of sixteen tracks had worked at any one time.

The gig, at least from what I've seen on film, was a complete bloody shambles, although we did actually enjoy it.

ABOVE:
Atlanta International Pop Festival poster, July 1969.

RIGHT:
Jimi at the Young Rascals concert, July 1969.

FAR RIGHT:
The band performing at Woodstock, August 1969. Jimi, Mitch (directly behind Jimi), Billy Cox, Larry Lee, Jerry Velez and Juma Sultan.

150

The other thing was that they found a girl's boarding school or a convent or something, where a lot of the film was shot. It was a terrible place, really depressing, especially when we came back from the gig. It's where they did the scenes of Jimi talking about out-of-the-body experiences and stuff. I think by this time Jimi wanted to have a bit of fun with the people involved; basically he thought that they were a bunch of wankers. Except I don't think it comes across that way on the film, it seems very serious, it wasn't meant to be.

The film, as a whole is terrible, almost the worst film I've ever seen. I fell asleep at the preview and embarrassed all and sundry by snoring. There again it's not the only Hendrix film I've snored through. I went to the premiere of Joe Boyd's film, with the star-studded audience and all that and I'd been in the studio for about three days and I was really tired. In fact virtually everything on film of Hendrix is terrible, but maybe the Gold and Goldstein stuff will be better if it ever surfaces.

We did a gig at the International Arena on Hawaii, the next day and then we didn't do anything else for about a month before the Isle of Wight. We hadn't even had a rehearsal and Jimi only arrived in London a day or so before the gig. I missed the opening party for Electric Lady Studios. In fact Jimi flew over virtually straight after the party, which is really sad, because it meant that outside of a few demos we put down while the studios were being completed, he never got to use his own studio.

I've heard it said that by the time it opened he was getting bored with recording and working in the studio, but it's really not true – it really was a dream for him having his own studio. Either way it was stupid that we didn't have some kind of play before the Isle of Wight. In actual fact we'd been playing quite well on the road, but to go in cold was a mistake. We were rusty and it showed.

The audience didn't help and we had technical problems, with funny voices coming through the PA. Anything like that,

Isle Of Wight Festival, East Afton Farm, IOW 30.8.70

The Queen (National Anthem); Sgt. Pepper; Spanish Castle Magic; All Along The Watchtower; Machine Gun; Lover Man; Freedom; Red House; Dolly Dagger; Midnight Lightning; Foxy Lady; Message To Love; Hey Baby; Ezy Rider; Hey Joe; Purple Haze; Voodoo Chile; In From The Storm.
Note: Many films exist of the Isle of Wight concert, some better than others, none really good. Also filmed segments appear in many rock compilation films. The soundboard recording was done by Pye, but several audience recordings exist and French radio recorded part of the concert.

Advert for Isle of Wight Festival, J.H.E. heading the bill for Sunday.

problems with the equipment – he could get upset, even if the fault was only temporary. The sound, in fact, wasn't too bad, but it was cold and dank – typical British weather, of course – but whatever the reasons it was just a lousy performance.

After the gig we jumped on a charter plane and headed for Sweden for the next show. I remember we were all really brought down by our performance, but Hendrix, in particular, seemed really tired.

So the next gig was in Stockholm, yet again. The gig itself was unmemorable. The next night was Gothenburg, which again was not bad, but there was something very bland about it. Also there was no real partying after the gig, no hanging out. Even Billy who'd never before been to any of these places, didn't seem terribly excited about it. That night I got a call from England, my

daughter Aysha had been born.

I chartered a plane and flew back to see Aysha, just for the day, in fact I saw her for about an hour. I got back just in time for the gig that night which was Aarhus in Denmark. I was tired, but really up. The gig was awful and Jimi left the stage after about two numbers. I don't know what went down with Jimi that day, because I'd been away, but something obviously had.

The next night in Copenhagen wasn't much better, although we finished the set – just grim. I don't think Jimi did sound-checks for those gigs, which was really odd. There was obviously something on his mind and he played just about the worst I'd ever heard him. Berlin, by contrast, was a lot better, for some reason. It was no great shakes, but by comparison with the previous two, it seemed almost a triumph.

Jimi, Mitch and Billy Cox at the Isle of Wight Festival.

Which brings us on to the 'Love and Peace Festival' on the Isle of Fehmarn, West Germany. What an extraordinary gig. I think we flew from Berlin to meet up with all the other bands. We then all took a train to the coast and finally a ferry to the island. It was a very early call first off, to get to the airport. Once there I got a lot of hassle from them about my passport, which I'd had for years. By this time I had long hair and didn't look much like the photo and they weren't going to let me through. It was early in the morning and I wasn't in the best of moods and rumour has it that I actually assaulted one of the guards. Thank God one of the promoters was there and between him and Stickells, they sorted everything out. So the day started well.

We got to the gig and all the bands were checked into the same hotel, probably the only hotel on the island. The people running the hotel didn't know what they had let themselves in for, the bands had completely taken over the place. We got there mid-afternoon and were supposedly on at eight. By about six we heard this wind and then it turned into a gale.

We knew by then that there were other problems as well. The usual equipment troubles plus bikers with guns and various militants. We knew we wouldn't play at eight, but we were told that we might get on by midnight. Well, we'd gone through Woodstock, so what's new? By mid-evening, because of the gale, none of the bands could play at all and they were all back at the hotel.

By nine o'clock the hotel had been drunk dry, fights were breaking out, all substances had been consumed. We're talking about a couple of hundred musicians, who were not having any fun. We sent some of the roadies out to the site to get some beer, which did ease the situation slightly. And, of course, two hundred musicians altogether and not working, it was, 'Let's party!' By midnight it was all getting too crazy for me, the bar had been wrecked and it was total lunacy. I didn't want anything to do with it, so I went up to my room.

Jimi and Billy Cox, Isle of Fehmarn Concert, September 1970.

I hadn't been there long, when I got a knock at the door and it's Billy, looking completely bewildered. By this time I'd spent nine months with him and he'd always been totally stable and reliable. He said, 'You know we're not going to get off this island alive. It's going to be taken over by the Nazis.'

He was in my room for three hours and although he was rambling, he made a certain amount of sense and many of his prophecies came true – odd. I called Jimi and we tried to calm him down. It was difficult to say what the problem was. He never took acid, in fact he rarely smoked, and although he might have been spiked, I think we would have known, you can tell if someone is tripping. We could probably have dealt with it better if it had been that.

To this day we don't know what happened to him, he was highly emotional and highly disturbed. We tried to find a doctor, which of course was impossible, but after several hours he did seem calmer and did get some sleep.

Anyway, because of the gale, we were rescheduled for midday on the Sunday. We heard that there had been real problems overnight – a lot of violence. We drove out to the site, got out of the car and this plank of wood with six-inch nails in it was thrown from the back of a group of Hell's Angels and

Jimi at the Isle of Wight rock festival, August 1970.

*A*nd, of course, two hundred musicians all together and not working, it was, 'Let's party!' By midnight it was all getting too crazy for me, the bar had been wrecked and it was total lunacy.

hit Gerry Stickells on the head. Fortunately, he got off lightly, but the feeling was, let's do the gig and get the hell out.

Our actual performance was OK and our adrenalin was pumping as well, but we did do a slightly shorter than usual set. We rushed off the stage, helicopter back to the mainland and straight back to England. We were glad to get out.

Some of Billy's prophecies did come true, people were killed and they did seal off the island after we left, for a couple of days. Also, and I found this out recently, one of our roadies, Rocky, was shot right through the leg by a machine gun, while taking down our equipment. One of those places with a really ugly feeling, a bit like The Stones gig at Altamont, I suppose.

So we got back to England and I have to say that Jimi was not too bright at this time, for whatever reason and he did seem depressed, although he'd been OK with Billy that night on the island. The night we got back, Billy started 'going' again and Jimi and Gerry took him to the doctor. The thought was that they hadn't seen paranoia like this for a long time, but induced by what, they and we didn't know. Maybe just the pressure of having been thrust into the limelight had built up over the months. We really didn't know. He did get better, but for a couple of weeks there, it was pretty frightening. We'd get in a cab and he'd say, 'No, no they're getting at me, it's a frame-up.'

Jimi spent quite a lot of time with Billy during that time. I think I only saw him for one day, as I was spending most of the time down at my house. The idea was that Billy should go home as soon as possible, as a result of which we had to cancel the last two gigs in Europe.

In that first week back on the Thursday, Jimi called me and told me he was OK and that he was doing some writing and looking forward to going back to New York and the new studio. We agreed that a new bass player was an inevitability and I suggested that it would be a smart move to conscript a few more musicians for the band and look

for a producer. We certainly talked about Jack Casady again and Jack Bruce was considered as well, but we figured that with the Cream connotation, he would probably not be too keen.

We talked about a couple of the old Motown players. Everbody we wanted seemed to be spoken for. Somebody told me recently Stephen Stills would have been up for it. That would have been wonderful; it's a shame we didn't know that. We also considered horn players and talked about calling up The Brecker Brothers, either to work with them or to ask them, at least, if they knew any hot young players that they could recommend.

I spent the next week taking care of bits and pieces down at my house and giving thought to possible musicians. I guess I was half expecting Jimi to ring and say, 'What about so and so?', but he never did. The following Thursday night, the 17th, I had to drive up to London. About quarter to seven I went to see Gerry Stickells, who said that Hendrix had called about fifteen minutes previously, would I give him a call?

I called him up and he asked me what I was doing. I told him I was just off to visit Ginger Baker and then we were going out to

Jimi, mid 1969.

Heathrow to meet Sly Stone, who was flying in.

Jimi was really excited about Sly and said, 'Is there any chance of a play?'

So I said, 'Funny you should say that, yeah, the idea is we're all going down to the Speakeasy for a jam.'

Jimi was really up for it and agreed to

Below:
Jimi, Band of Gypsys Concert 1970.

meet us there about midnight. His agreeing was no surprise: anywhere in the world, Jimi was always up for a play; it took precedence over anything.

Anyway, we met Sly, who was knocked out that Jimi wanted to play and after checking him in at the hotel, we went down to the club. We got there and we waited and we waited. By one o'clock people were starting to sort of look at each other and by two they were starting to say it was odd.

In the end we all sat there till closing time which was about four. I remember having this odd feeling when I left that was hard to define. If nothing else it was just so out of character for Hendrix not to have shown, especially as he'd appeared full of beans earlier and really wanted to do it.

I drove back to my house, about an hour and a half's drive. I didn't go to bed and sat up for what seemed like a few hours, but may well have been longer. I'm not sure of the time, but I got a call from Eric Barrett, telling me that Jimi had died. I just couldn't believe it. I couldn't release any emotion at all. I finally got some sleep about six the next night, but waking up later, it was a bit like when Jimi had crashed his car in Benedict Canyon and had come in and told me about it, you know, 'Did I dream that?'

Again I woke up thinking 'Was that the truth?' and, of course, sadly it was. I couldn't handle it at all.

The worst thing was the funeral, it was like a circus. I flew out to Seattle with Noel, who I'd seen a few times in the past months. He hadn't seen much of Jimi, but he had been to the opening of the Electric Lady studio and there was still a lot of affection between all of us.

In Seattle most of us were staying in the same hotel and in all honesty it felt like a gig. There was a knock at the door in the morning and Gerry Stickells stood there and said, 'It's time to go now,' and I'm sure I said, 'What time's the gig?' I know it sounds sick, but maybe that was the only way I could deal with it. It was OK until we got to the church and you realized what kind of event the powers that be had made this.

I think it started to hit me during the service, especially when we had to walk up the aisle and file past the open coffin. Neither Noel nor I had been through anything like that before. God, it was the most awful thing, Noel and I held hands – that was when it really hit home.

One small side event of the day of the funeral happened before we left to go to the church. I'd heard that Buddy Miles, maybe incorrectly, but I don't think so, was slagging me off as some kind of racist pig who had a thing against blacks. I lost my rag completely. I went to his room and put him up on the wall, there's like eight and half stone of me. So I held him up there and said, 'Don't you fucking dare!'

I'd been nothing else but kind to him, as had Jimi, which is more than I can say about some of his attitudes over the years. He started apologizing and said, 'Maybe you heard it wrongly.' He didn't say that it wasn't true.

They'd booked the Seattle Coliseum or somewhere, for the wake, a place we'd played, certainly. It was really gauche, but probably not a bad idea in retrospect. People got up and played, Noel and I did play later in the day, but I kept a pretty low profile and got an early flight home. It was one of the worst days of my life. Even after I got home it was hard to accept that he was dead; it still felt as though he was right there.

Ultimately, of course, nothing can alter the fact that on September 18 1970, at 11.45 a.m. Jimi Hendrix was admitted to St Mary Abbot's Hospital in London and that at 12.15 p.m. he was officially pronounced dead. The verdict was inhalation of vomit. The only drug content found at the autopsy was quinal barbitone, more commonly known as seconal, approximately nine tablets.

What led up to Jimi's death remains a matter of speculation and is unlikely ever to be fully explained. Suicide is generally ruled out, although he wasn't going through a wonderfully happy period, and foul play seems more the stuff of conspiracy theories, which leaves 'accidental death' as the most likely cause.

The whole thing with the night Jimi died is odd. There are definitely a couple of hours in there that no one can account for. We know that he went to see Alan Douglas, who was in town, likewise Devon Wilson. Devon was staying in Mayfair, not far from the Speakeasy, so I can see him going there to pick her up en route to the club.

Earlier on in the evening Jimi is supposed to have got stuck in traffic at Marble Arch and talked to people in an adjacent car, who invited him to a party, which he ultimately went to. I find that very odd as well. At some point, later on, he definitely phoned someone – Gerry, I think – in the course of which he said something like, 'I'll never do that again,' but what that referred to I don't know.

Jimi was spending most of those last days with Monika Danneman, who – no offence to her – was not the great love of Jimi's life. There had only really been two of these, Cathy Etchingham in the early days in England and Devon Wilson. I do know, though, that Devon was becoming a bit of a handful by then and he wasn't overjoyed to discover she was over here as well. Sadly Devon died under mysterious circumstances herself a few years later.

What did happen we'll probably never know. I certainly don't think it was suicide. Undoubtedly he'd been tired and depressed, especially after those last European gigs, but definitely not suicidal. I think it was a tragic accident, but some of the circumstances surrounding it are certainly odd.

In the end all you can say is, 'What a fucking waste.' He was irreplaceable, both as a friend and musician. I miss him as much today as twenty years ago. There was so much more that he was capable of and his music would have changed as would the musicians he worked with, including drummers. I like to think, though, not that I *was* the perfect drummer for Jimi, but that maybe once a year we'd always get together to do some gigs, each of us having played with other people in the mean time. There is no doubt, though, that he was not simply a hard act to follow – more an impossible act to follow.

*October 1, 1970 Seattle,
Washington, U.S.A.*

*W hat did happen we'll probably never know. I certainly don't
think it was suicide. He'd certainly been tired and depressed,
especially after those last European gigs, but definitely not suicidal.
I think it was a tragic accident, but some of the circumstances
surrounding it are certainly odd.*

CRY of LOVE

THE CRY OF LOVE Track 2408 101 (mid. 71)

US Reprise RS 2034

SIDE 1 Freedom; Drifting; Ezy Ryder; Night Bird Flying; My Friend.

SIDE 2 Straight Ahead; Astro Man; Angel; In From The Storm; Belly Button Window.

All tracks written by Jimi Hendrix.
Produced by Jimi Hendrix; Mitch Mitchell & Eddie Kramer.

OPPOSITE:
Irreplaceable and completely unique – Jimi Hendrix.

WHEN ANY MAJOR RECORDING ARTIST DIES, those people who control his or her recorded product are faced with an inevitable dilemma. What work should be issued (or re-issued), in what form and – more to the point – when?

If work is issued very quickly after an artist's death, then the public, justifiably or not, will cry that their beloved hero's memory is being cruelly exploited for commercial ends. If the powers-that-be leave it too long, then they run the risk of the public 'forgetting' the artist. Equally they may feel, probably quite rightly, that they have a duty with regard to the artist's 'legacy' and the respecting of his 'wishes' with regard to material that would have been issued and was only prevented from being so by his death.

There is also the duty to the family of the deceased to ensure that the artist continues to act as a 'breadwinner' even after his death, a concept in which there is nothing inherently immoral. Lastly, of course, there is the thorny area of the public's right of access to the artist's material. At what point does one say 'No, the artist did not record this or that piece for public consumption?'

These problems and others, surround the deaths of all major artists, Hendrix no less than others. Most artists leave a small body of unreleased material, usually a few outtakes from albums, the odd concert and perhaps an un-

finished, but clearly defined final record. In Hendrix's case it was estimated that there was anything from 500 to 1,000 hours of unreleased material, including things that may or may not have been part of a 'last' album. In the case of studio material (easily the bulk of the tapes) the tapes contained anything and everything from one guitar part right up to virtually finished recordings, whether they were songs or just loose jams.

Ultimately the responsibility for decisions regarding the Hendrix archive became the responsibility of the Hendrix Estate, but in the early days after Hendrix's death Mike Jeffery was still involved. He made the bright decision that if an album was going to be done (and one can't escape the fact that it was in his interest, if no one else's, to see that it was) then it should be Mitch and Hendrix's old engineer, Eddie Kramer, who should put it together. Considering the circumstances, however, it was no easy decision to work on the project.

I don't remember how long after Jimi's funeral it was, but I got a call from Jeffery, not that long probably. What he said was that there were only two people who knew the material, myself and Eddie Kramer. How did I feel about coming over to New York, to go through the tapes? The honest answer was that I didn't know. I thought it over and said that I'd go over for a couple of days, give it a try and see how it feels. So that's what I did.

LEFT:
Jimi's presence was strong as ever in the studio – Cry of Love, 1970.

'*C*ry of Love' as the album ended up being called, was a real jigsaw puzzle to put together. You'd find, say, a lead guitar part in one key and then a vocal and rhythm track for the same song in a different key and one had to be speeded up or slowed down to match the other. It was bare bones stuff, without a doubt.

The studio had changed since I'd last seen it. I hadn't been there for the opening and hadn't seen it since it had been more than about half finished. Jimi had seen it more or less finished like the murals on the stairs, that kind of thing, although there were still some last-minute things being carried out when I went back, including bits of the outboard. Surprisingly, it didn't feel too bad. There had been a very good chance that I wouldn't have been able to deal with it at all, particularly so close to Jimi's death, but it was OK, felt quite warm. I saw Mike and Eddie and said that I'd do it.

So we started to work on the material. Our first problem was that it turned out that Electric Lady only had about half of the existing tapes. Primarily it was stuff that had been done there as demos before its official opening, plus material recorded in various studios in New York over the few months prior to that. Most of the remaining tapes, material going back as far as early 1968, if not before, was at Warner Bros. It became obvious that they had material that we would have wanted but for whatever reason – and I never really knew what it was – we weren't allowed near them. There is no doubt that the album we did put together would have been better and easier to produce if we could have used some of that stuff.

Anyway we got to work on what we had. We worked from about nine at night till about seven in the morning. I'd have a shower and kip down on the floor – I did that for several weeks.

'Cry of Love' as the album ended up being called, was a real jigsaw puzzle to put together. You'd find, say, a lead guitar part in one key and then a vocal and rhythm track for the same song in a different key and one had to be speeded up or slowed down to match the other. It was bare bones stuff, without a doubt. Of course it would have been different if Hendrix had been working on it. I have no doubt that he would have scrapped quite a lot of the stuff that was there and started some things all over again. There again, there were bits I know he could have kept.

ABOVE:
Billy Cox in the studio
1970.

RIGHT:
Stephen Stills – a good
friend to Jimi and a
great musician!

*W*ithout being cosmic, which I'm not, I did keep getting these
incredibly vivid dreams, to the point of visitations and
conversations. What do you think of this mix? And he'd tell me.
Reality? Who knows.

Jimi playing drums.

BELOW:
Mitch at London's Hard Rock Cafe holding Jimi's favourite guitar, the white Fender stratocaster used at Woodstock and Isle of Wight. The guitar was sold at Sotheby's, London 1990, for £198,000 or roughly $340,000.

Basically I tried to think of what he would have done, or what he would have wanted, which was a very difficult thing to do. If something worked I left it, like Buddy Miles' drum part on 'Ezy Rider'. It could have been dropped and replaced with one by me – but it was fine so I left it. At no point did I get a bad feeling working in the studio. Without being cosmic, which I'm not, I did keep getting these incredibly vivid dreams, to the point of visitations and conversations. 'What do you think of this mix?' And he'd tell me. Reality? Who knows.

I wish, in retrospect we'd had more time to work on the record. Mike's office was upstairs and he was obviously trying to turn the studio into a commercially viable set-up, with outside bookings. So little by little it became more difficult to find time to work on things. As I said, I always tried hard to think of what Jimi would have wanted, not just his parts, but what else he would have wanted.

On 'Drifting' we had two guitar tracks. One had gone through the univerb 'Leslie' effect and I think we had another one in another key. So we dropped the speed on it, put that through the Leslie, mixed and matched and got some stereo going. I just felt that vibes would be perfect for some background feeling and I know Jimi would have liked it. So I got Buzzy Linhart in for a session on vibes and it worked and I was really pleased with it.

The harmonica player on 'My Friend'

remains a mystery. It's on the original track, but no one could remember who played it. After we'd finished the record this guy Gers phoned up and said, 'Don't forget I played harmonica', so we gave him a credit, but it could have been anybody. I'm fairly certain that there are other background vocalists on 'In From The Storm' besides Emerelta Marks, including Ronnie Spector and myself. I'd always give it a go, stand there with your finger in your ear – loosen the tonsils. No big deal until the next day when you suddenly realize that you really were singing with Mavis Staples or whoever.

It became apparent fairly quickly when we were going through the tapes that a couple of drum overdubs were essential, especially on 'Angel'. It was weird, Stephen Stills was working in studio B next door and, of course, he knew Hendrix well. So we had him come in and check my new parts out. They were my drum parts originally, but either they were too scrappy or after the inevitable transfers and speed changes they needed beefing up.

Actually it's funny about the drum kit I used. Hendrix was always destroying guitars and at Woodstock, I said, 'I'll have this one before it gets destroyed' meaning the white Stratocaster he'd used at Woodstock. I'd given him a drum kit for Electric Lady, an old Gretsch I'd used at Berkeley. So I said to him 'I'll have that guitar before you smash it' and he said 'Sure, you got it.' It was a bit of a joke exchange and doing the overdubs was the first time I'd seen that drum kit since I'd given it to him – it felt strange. I suppose it's kind of irony that 'Angel' was the most difficult and jigsaw-like track to put together and yet it became the most coveted of Jimi's songs.

In retrospect I feel proud of 'Cry Of Love'. I think we did the best we could using the tapes we had. If Warner's had been co-operative and we'd had more time, it would certainly have been better. I think it's undoubtedly better than many of the later albums, which even with access to the other tapes, leave a lot to be desired.

As to what Hendrix himself would have wanted to release is obviously a matter of speculation. I know that it would have been along the lines of 'Cry Of Love', but just as we would have used some of the other tapes, if we could have got them, so would he. Of course, if he'd lived, then access would obviously not have been a problem. He probably wouldn't have called it 'Cry Of Love'. It was his title, but where we came across it, I'm not sure. It may have been in some of his notes or a working title for a song – I honestly can't remember. He'd toyed with various titles like 'The First Rays Of The New Rising Sun', but who knows if he would ever have used that in the end?

Clearly though 'Cry Of Love', or whatever variation he would finally have released, was not the only album he'd been contemplating. The Gil Evans orchestrated album, with or without Miles Davis, I'm sure would have happened; likewise an acoustic album – probably a blues-based one.

We did a lot of recordings at home – me on brushes, phone books etc., Hendrix on his favourite Martin acoustic – which haven't been released, but then they weren't supposed to be. I'm sure he would have gone into the studio at some point to record some of that stuff properly, possibly with someone like Taj Mahal. In fact he did do some informal recording with Taj.

I wouldn't mind betting that he would also have done a full-out rock 'n' roll album, mixing covers and original material, but what might have been the most interesting project of all was a collaboration with Quincy Jones. Quincy first met Jimi when we were living in LA and he came out to visit us in Benedict Canyon and later on in 1970 he came to see the band at the Forum. I don't think anything definite was planned, but I know Quincy was up for it and Hendrix always had it in the back of his mind. What a shame it never happened.

It's just so sad and frustrating that none of these projects – and who knows what else – ever happened. I'm just glad that he produced as much as he did and the existence of any number of later releases of dubious quality can never detract from that.

JAMES MARSHALL HENDRIX
27th November 1942–
18th September 1970.

THERE IS MORE INTEREST TODAY IN HENDRIX and his work than at any time since the height of his career. Young people who were hardly born at the time of his death cite him as their favourite artist; fan clubs and newsletters about him thrive and there is at least one museum dedicated to him. Many fine young guitar players, notably Robert Cray, cite Jimi as a primary influence and thousands of aspiring players pore over transcriptions of his guitar parts, hoping for a little of the magic to rub off.

Hendrix, then wasn't just a 'Sixties' artist even in the most general sense. He certainly can't be tied to any of the Sixties musical movements – the Blues Revival, Acid Rock, Heavy Metal or anything else. And therein lies his enduring quality: his music – like the man himself – belonged to any place, at any time and there are precious few artists about whom that can be said.

SET LISTS

Blaises, Queensgate, London 21.12.66

Rock Me Baby; Third Stone From the Sun; Like A Rolling Stone; Hey Joe; Wild Thing. (Possibly other titles as well)

Flamingo, Wardour St., London 4.2.67

Killing Floor; Have Mercy; Can You See Me; Like A Rolling Stone; Rock Me Baby; Catfish Blues; Stone Free; Hey Joe; Wild Thing.

The BBC Recordings

Saturday Club: 15.2.67 (recording date)
Stone Free; Love Or Confusion; Hey Joe; Foxy Lady.
Saturday Club: 27.3.67 (recording date)
Killing Floor; Fire; Purple Haze.
Top Gear 6.10.67 (recording date)
Radio One Theme; Catfish Blues; Driving South; Hound Dog; Burning Of The Midnight Lamp; Little Miss Lover; I Was Born To Love Her/Midnight Hour

Star Club, Hamburg 17.3.67

Foxy Lady; Hey Joe; Stone Free; Fire; Purple Haze. (Possibly others)

Astoria, Finsbury Park, London 31.3.67

Foxy Lady; Can You See Me; Hey Joe; Purple Haze.

Alexis Korner's Rhythm And Blues Show 17.10.67 (recording date)

Catfish Blues; Can You Please Crawl Out Your Window; Hoochie Koochie Man; Driving South.

Top Gear 15.12.67 (recording date)

Day Tripper; Wait Until Tomorrow; Spanish Castle Magic; Hear My Train A Comin'.
Note: These were not the only sessions that The Experience recorded for the BBC, but they are the only ones that remain in the archives.

Swedish Radio Broadcast, Stockholm 5.9.67

Sgt. Pepper's Lonely Hearts Club Band; Hey Joe; I Don't Live Today; Burning Of The Midnight Lamp; Purple Haze; The Wind Cries Mary; Foxy Lady; Fire.

Olympia, Paris 9.10.67

Foxy Lady; Wind Cries Mary; Rock Me Baby; Red House; Purple Haze; Wild Thing; Hey Joe.

Opera House, Blackpool 25.11.67

Sgt. Pepper; Fire; Hey Joe; Wind Cries Mary; Purple Haze; Wild Thing.

Falkonner Hall (or Theatre), Copenhagen 7.1.68

Sgt. Pepper; Fire; Hey Joe; The Wind Cries Mary; Purple Haze; Spanish Castle Magic; Catfish Blues; Wild Thing.

Olympia, Paris 29.1.68

Killing Floor; Catfish Blues; Foxy Lady; Red House; The Wind Cries Mary; Driving South; Fire; Little Wing; Purple Haze.

State Fair Music Hall, Dallas 16.2.68

Are You Experienced; Fire; The Wind Cries Mary; Tax Free; Foxy Lady; Hey Joe; Spanish Castle Magic; Red House; Purple Haze.

Will Rogers Auditorium, Forth Worth, Texas 17.2.68

Sgt. Pepper; Can You Please Crawl Out Your Window; The Wind Cries Mary; Fire; Catfish Blues; Foxy Lady; Hey Joe; Purple Haze.

Auditorium, Montreal 2.4.68

Killing Floor; Hey Joe; Fire; The Wind Cries Mary; Foxy Lady; I Don't Live Today; Manic Depression; Purple Haze; Wild Thing.

Singer Bowl, New York 23.8.68

Are You Experienced; Fire; Red House; I Don't Live Today; Foxy Lady; Like A Rolling Stone; Purple Haze; Hey Joe; Wild Thing.

Philharmonic Hall, New York 28.11.68

Fire; I Don't Live Today; Hear My Train; Spanish Castle Magic; Foxy Lady; Red House; Sunshine Of Your Love; Purple Haze.

Konserthus, Stockholm, Sweden 9.1.69

First Show: Killing Floor; Spanish Castle Magic; Fire; Hey Joe; Voodoo Chile; Red House; Sunshine Of Your Love.
2nd Show: I Don't Live Today; Spanish Castle Magic; Hey Joe; Voodoo Chile; Sunshine Of Your Love; Red House.
Note: The first show was filmed by Swedish Television.

Forum, Los Angeles 26.4.69

Tax Free; Foxy Lady; Red House; Spanish Castle Magic; Star Spangled Banner; Purple Haze; I Don't Live Today; Voodoo Chile; Sunshine Of Your Love.

Maple Leaf Gardens, Toronto 3.5.69

Fire; Hear My Train; Spanish Castle Magic; Red House; Foxy Lady; Blues Jam; Purple Haze; Voodoo Chile.
Note: The Blues Jam is just that, featuring lyrics from Room Full Of Mirrors, Crash Landing, Keep On Groovin', Gypsy Eyes.

Sports Arena, San Diego, California 24.5.69

Hey Joe; Spanish Castle Magic; Red House; Fire; I Don't Live Today; Star Spangled Banner; Foxy Lady; Purple Haze; Voodoo Chile.

The Band of Gypsys Concerts

Fillmore East, New York – 31.12.69 – 1st Show
Power Of Soul; Lover Man; Hear My Train; Them Changes; Izabella; Machine Gun; Stop; Ezy Ryder; Bleeding Heart; Earth Blues; Burning Desire.
Fillmore East, New York – 31.12.69 – 2nd Show
Auld Lang Syne; Who Knows; Stepping Stone; Burning Desire; Fire; Ezy Ryder; Machine Gun; Power Of Soul; Stone Free/Sunshine Of Your Love; Them Changes; Message To Love; Stop; Foxy Lady; Voodoo Chile; Purple Haze.
Fillmore East, New York – 1.1.70 – 1st Show
Who Knows; Machine Gun; Them Changes; Power Of Soul; Stepping Stone; Foxy Lady; Stop; Earth Blues.
Fillmore East, New York – 1.1.70 – 2nd Show
Them Changes; Power Of Soul; Message To Love; Earth Blues; Machine Gun; Voodoo Chile; We Gotta Live Together; Wild Thing; Hey Joe; Purple Haze.

Forum, Los Angeles 25.4.70

Spanish Castle Magic; Foxy Lady; Lover Man; Hear My Train A Comin'; Message To Love; Ezy Rider; Machine Gun; Room Full Of Mirrors; Star Spangled Banner; Voodoo Chile.

Community Center, Berkeley, California 30.5.70

1st Show: Fire; Johnny B. Goode; Hear My Train A Comin'; Foxy Lady; Machine Gun; Freedom; Message To Love; Red House; Ezy Rider; Star Spangled Banner; Purple Haze; Voodoo Chile.
2nd Show: Straight Ahead; Hey Baby; Lover Man; Stone Free; Hey Joe; I Don't Live Today; Machine Gun; Foxy Lady; Star Spangled Banner; Purple Haze; Voodoo Chile.

New York Pop Festival, Randalls Island, New York 17.7.70

Stone Free; Fire; Red House; Message To Love; Look Over Yonder; All Along The Watchtower; Foxy Lady; Ezy Rider; Star Spangled Banner; Purple Haze.

Gröna Lund Stockholm 31.8.70

Lover Man; Catfish Blues/Race With The Devil (short inst. jam); Ezy Ryder; Red House; Come On; Room Full Of Mirrors; Hey Baby; Message To Love; Machine Gun; Voodoo Chile; In From The Storm; Purple Haze; Foxy Lady.

Isle Of Fehmarn 6.9.70

Killing Floor; Spanish Castle Magic; Foxy Lady; All Along The Watchtower; Hey Joe; Hey Baby; Ezy Ryder; Freedom, Room Full Of Mirrors; Purple Haze; Voodoo Chile; Message To Love.

TOUR ITINERARY

Concerts, club dates, T.V. appearances and other significant dates

1966

OCTOBER
Wed 5 Jimi, Mitch and Noel play together for the first time
Thu 13 Evreux, France (opening for Johnny Halliday)
Fri 14 Nancy, France
Sat 15 Reims, France
Sun 16 Luxembourg, Grand Duchy of Luxembourg
Tue 18 L'Olympia, Paris
Tue 25 Scotch of St. James, London (private showcase for J.H.E)

NOVEMBER
Tue 8 Big Apple Club, Munich, West Germany
Wed 9 Big Apple Club, Munich, West Germany (Jimi smashes guitar up for the first time.)
Thu 10 Big Apple Club, Munich, West Germany
Fri 25 Bag O'Nails, Soho, London
Sat 26 Ricky Tick, Hounslow, U.K.
Sun 27 Jimi's 24th birthday

DECEMBER
Sat 10 Ram Jam Club, Brixton, London
Tue 13 Recorded first T.V. programme, 'Ready Steady Go!'
Fri 16 Transmission first J.H.E. T.V. appearance on 'Ready Steady Go!' – U.K., "Hey Joe" performed. Live at Chislehurst Caves, U.K.
Wed 21 Blaises Club, Queensgate, London
Thu 22 Southampton, U.K.
Fri 23 Ricky Tick Club
Mon 26 Upper Cut Club, East End, London
Thu 29 'Top of the Pops', BBC-TV show, London
Sat 31 Stan's, Folkestone, U.K. (also known as Toft's)

1967

JANUARY
Wed 4 Bromel Club, Bromley Court Hotel, Bromley, U.K.
Sat 7 New Century Hall, Manchester, U.K.
Sun 8 Mojo Club, Sheffield, U.K.
Wed 11 Bag O'Nails, London
Thu 12 7½ Club, Mayfair, London
Fri 13 7½ Club, Mayfair, London
Sat 14 Beachcomber Club, Nottingham, U.K.
Sun 15 Kirklevington, outside Middlesbrough, U.K.
Mon 16 7½ Club, Mayfair, London
Tue 17 7½ Club, Mayfair, London
Wed 18 7½ Club and Top of the Pops, BBC-TV, London
Thu 19 Speakeasy
Fri 20 Haverstock Hill Country Club, Hampstead London
Sat 21 Refectory, Golders Green, London
Sun 22 The Astoria, Oldham, U.K.
Tue 24 Marquee Club, London
Wed 25 Oxford Cellar, Norwich, U.K.
Fri 27 Chislehurst Caves, Chislehurst, U.K.
Sat 28 Upper Cut Club, London
Sun 29 Saville Theatre, London (with The Who)
Tue 31 Saville Theatre, London (film shoot)

FEBRUARY
Wed 1 Cellar Club, South Shields, U.K.
Thu 2 Top of the Pops BBC-TV, ("Purple Haze") Live: Imperial Club, Darlington, U.K.
Fri 3 Ricky Tick Club, Hounslow, U.K.
Sat 4 Ram Jam Club, Brixton, London
Sun 5 Flamingo, (All Nighter Club), London
Mon 6 Star Hotel, Croydon, U.K.
Wed 8 Bromel Club, Bromley, U.K.
Thu 9 Locarno Club, Bristol, U.K.
Fri 10 Ricky Tick, Newbury, U.K.
Sat 11 Blue Moon, Cheltenham, U.K.
Sun 12 Sinking Ship, Stockport, U.K.
Mon 13 Saturday Club Radio Show (BBC)
Tue 14 Gray's Club, Tilbury, U.K.
Wed 15 Dorothy's Ballroom, Cambridge, U.K.
Fri 17 Ricky Tick, Windsor, U.K.
Sat 18 University of York, York, U.K.
Sun 19 Brady's Club, London
Mon 20 The Pavilion, Bath, U.K.
Tue 21 Bornemouth, U.K.
Wed 22 Roundhouse, Chalk Farm, London
Thu 23 Pier Pavilion, Worthing, U.K.
Fri 24 University of Leicester, Leicester, U.K.
Sat 25 Corn Exchange, Chelmsford, U.K.
Sun 26 St. Mary Cray, U.K.

MARCH
Wed 1 Orchid Ballroom, Purley, U.K.
Thu 2 Marquee Club, London
Sat 4 La Faculte de Droit D'assas, Graduation Ball, Paris, France
Mon 6 Brussels, Belgium, TV appearance
Wed 8 Speakeasy, London
Thu 9 Skyline Hotel, Hull, U.K.
Fri 10 Club A Go Go, Newcastle-upon-Tyne, U.K.
Sat 11 International Club, Leeds, U.K.
Sun 12 Gyro Club, Ilkley, U.K. (Show stopped: fire code violations)
Mon 13 J.H.E. fly to Amsterdam
Tue 14 Recorded 'Fan Club' Dutch TV show live Amsterdam, Holland
Wed 15 Film 'Beat Club', West German TV Show
Fri 17 Star Club, Hamburg, Germany
Sat 18 Star Club, Hamburg, Germany
Sun 19 Star Club, Hamburg, Germany
Tue 21 Speakeasy, London
Wed 22 Guildhall, Southampton, U.K.
Sat 25 Gliderdrome, Boston, U.K.
Sun 26 Tabernacle Club, Stockport, U.K.
Tue 28 Market Hall, Aylesbury, U.K.
Thu 30 Top of the Pops, BBC-TV
Fri 31 Start of first official J.H.E. Tour of U.K. with Walker Bros, Cat Stevens, Engelbert Humperdinck. Finsbury Park Astoria, London

(it was at this gig Hendrix first set fire to his guitar.) (2 shows)

APRIL
Sat 1 Odeon, Ipswich, U.K. (2 shows)
Sun 2 Gaumont, Worcester U.K. (2 shows)
Tue 4 DeeTime T.V. show, BBC
Wed 5 Odeon, Leeds, U.K. (2 shows)
Thu 6 Odeon, Glasgow, Scotland (2 shows)
Fri 7 A.B.C., Carlisle, U.K. (2 shows)
Sat 8 A.B.C., Chesterfield, U.K. (2 shows)
Sun 9 Empire, Liverpool, U.K. (2 shows)
Tue 11 Granada, Bedford, U.K. (2 shows)
Wed 12 Gaumont, Southampton, U.K. (2 shows)
Thu 13 Odeon, Wolverhampton, U.K. (2 shows)
Fri 14 Odeon, Bolton, U.K. (2 shows)
Sat 15 Odeon, Blackpool, U.K. (2 shows)
Sun 16 De Montfort Hall, Leicester, U.K. (2 shows)
Mon 17 Luton, U.K. (2 shows)
Wed 19 Odeon, Birmingham, U.K. (2 shows)
Thu 20 A.B.C., Lincoln, U.K. (2 shows)
Fri 21 City Hall, Newcastle, U.K. (2 shows)
Sat 22 Odeon, Manchester, U.K. (2 shows)
Sun 23 Gaumont, Hanley, U.K. (2 shows)
Tue 25 Colston Hall, Bristol, U.K. (2 shows)
Wed 26 Capitol, Cardiff, Wales (2 shows)
Thu 27 A.B.C., Aldershot, U.K. (2 shows)
Fri 28 Adelphi, Slough, U.K. (2 shows)
Sat 29 Winter Gardens, Bournemouth, U.K. (2 shows)
Sun 30 Granada, Tooting, London (2 shows)

MAY
Thu 4 'Top of the Pops' BBC-TV
Sat 6 Imperial Ballroom, Nelson, U.K.
Sun 7 Saville Theatre, London (2 shows)
Mon 8 Speakeasy, London (Mitch and Jimi)
Wed 10 'Top of the Pops' BBC-TV
Thu 11 'Music Hall of France' (Paris TV show)
Fri 12 Bluesville Club, Manor House, London
Sat 13 Imperial College, Kensington, London
Sun 14 Belle Vue, Manchester, U.K.
Mon 15 Berlin, Germany (2 shows)
Tue 16 Munich, W. Germany (2 shows)
Wed 17 Frankfurt, W. Germany (2 shows)
Fri 19 Gothenburg, Sweden (2 shows)
Sat 20 Karlstaad, Sweden (2 shows)
Sun 21 Sports Arena, Copenhagen, Denmark
Mon 22 Kulttiiri Talo, Helsinki, Finnish TV show (afternoon), Finland
Tue 23 Bongo Club, Malmo, Sweden
Wed 24 Gröna Lund, Stockholm, Sweded
Thu 25 Sports Arena, Copenhagen, Denmark
Fri 26 Kiel, W. Germany
Sat 27 Braunsweig, W. Germany
Mon 29 Tulip Bulb Auction Hall, Spalding, U.K.

JUNE
Sun 4 Saville Theatre, London (2 shows)
Tue 13 Experience fly to New York
Thu 15 Fly to San Francisco

Sat 17 Rehearsals for Monterey Pop Festival
Sun 18 Monterey Pop Festival – J.H.E. first U.S. appearance
Tue 20 Fillmore West, San Francisco, (2 shows)
Wed 21 Fillmore West, San Francisco, (2 shows)
Thu 22 Fillmore West, San Francisco, (2 shows)
Fri 23 Fillmore West, San Francisco, (2 shows)
Sat 24 Fillmore West, San Francisco, (2 shows)
Sun 25 Afternoon: Golden Gate Park, San Francisco Free Concert
Evening: Fillmore West, San Francisco, (2 shows)

JULY

Sat 1 Earl Warren Showgrounds, Santa Barbara, California
Sun 2 Whiskey A Go Go, Los Angeles
Mon 3 Scene Club, New York City
Tue 4 Scene Club, New York City
Wed 5 Central Park, New York City, with The Young Rascals
Fri 7 J.H.E. to start Monkees Tour
Sat 8 Jacksonville, Florida
Sun 9 Jackie Gleason Memorial Hall, Miami (Mitch's 21st Birthday) Florida
Tue 11 Coliseum, Charlotte, North Carolina
Wed 12 Greensboro, North Carolina
Fri 14 Forest Hills, New York
Sat 15 Forest Hills, New York
Sun 16 Forest Hills, New York (J.H.E. off Monkees Tour)
Tue 18 Gaslight Club, Greenwich Village, N.Y.
Wed 19 Gaslight Club, Greenwich Village, N.Y.
Thu 20 Salvation Club, New York City
Fri 21 Cafe-a-Go-Go, New York City
Sat 22 Cafe-a-Go-Go, New York City
Sun 23 Cafe-a-Go-Go, New York City

AUGUST

Thu 3 Salvation Club, New York City
Fri 4 Salvation Club, New York City
Sat 5 Salvation Club, New York City
Mon 7 Salvation Club, New York City
Tue 8 Salvation Club, New York City
Wed 9 Ambassador Theatre, Washington D.C.
Thu 10 Ambassador Theatre, Washington D.C. (Mitch ill, show cancelled)
Fri 11 Ambassador Theatre, (Mitch back) Washington D.C.
Sat 12 Ambassador Theatre, Washington D.C.
Sun 13 Ambassador Theatre, Washington D.C.
Tue 15 Fifth Dimension Club, Ann Arbor, Michigan
Fri 18 Hollywood Bowl
Sat 19 Earl Warren Showground, Santa Barbara, Calif.
Mon 21 Experience return to London
Tue 22 Simon Dee Show, BBC-TV
Thu 24 Top of the Pops – BBC-TV
Sun 27 Saville Theatre, London (2nd Show cancelled, Brian Epstein's death)
Tue 29 Boat House Club, Nottingham, U.K.
Thu 31 Inn Club, London

SEPTEMBER

Sat 2 Berlin, West Germany
Sun 3 Liseburg, Gothenburg, Sweden
Mon 4 Gröna Lund, Stockholm, Sweden
Tue 5 Radiohaus, Stockholm (live performance broadcast), Sweden
Wed 6 Versteras, Sweden
Fri 8 Hogbo, Sweden
Sat 9 Karlstaad, Sweden
Sun 10 Malmo, Sweden
Mon 11 Gröna Lund, Stockholm (2 shows)
Tue 12 Gothenburg, Sweden

Thu 14 'Top of the Pops' BBC-TV
Fri 15 Manor House, London (Jimi and Mitch)
Mon 18 'Monday, Monday' Radio Show, London
Mon 25 'Guitar-In', Royal Festival Hall, London
Thu 28 Upper Cut, London (Jimi and Mitch)

OCTOBER

Fri 6 Top Gear Radio Show (jam with Stevie Wonder)
Sat 7 Wellington Club, Dereham, U.K.
Sun 8 Saville Theatre (2 shows), London
Mon 9 L'Olympia, Paris
Tue 10 Paris TV show
Fri 13 Jonathan King TV Show, A.T.V., U.K.
Sun 15 Crawley, U.K. (probably Starlight Ballroom)
Sun 22 Pier Pavilion, Hastings, U.K.
Tue 24 Marquee Club, London
Sat 28 California Hall, Dunstable, U.K.

NOVEMBER

Wed 8 Manchester University, Manchester, U.K.
Fri 10 Day TV show, Bussem, Holland
Ahoy Hal, Rotterdam, Holland
Sat 11 Brighton Dome, Brighton, U.K.
Tue 14 Royal Albert Hall, London (start of tour with Pink Floyd etc.)
Wed 15 Winter Gardens, Bournemouth, U.K. (2 shows)
Fri 17 City Hall, Sheffield, U.K. (2 shows)
Sat 18 Empire Theatre, Liverpool, U.K. (2 shows)
Sun 19 Coventry Theatre, Coventry, U.K. (2 shows)
Wed 22 Guildhall, Portsmouth, U.K. (2 shows)
Thu 23 Sophia Gardens, Cardiff, Wales (2 shows)
Fri 24 Colston Hall, Bristol, U.K. (2 shows)
Sat 25 Opera House, Blackpool, U.K. (filmed by BBC) 2 shows
Sun 26 Palace Theatre, Manchester, U.K. (2 shows)
Mon 27 Whitla Hall, Queen's College, Belfast, Northern Ireland (2 shows)

DECEMBER

Fri 1 Town Hall, Chatham, U.K. (2 shows)
Sat 2 The Dome, Brighton, U.K. (2 shows)
Sun 3 Theatre Royal, Nottingham, U.K. (2 shows)
Mon 4 City Hall, Newscastle, U.K. (2 shows)
Tue 5 Green's Playhouse, Glasgow, Scotland (2 shows)
Fri 8 'Jonathan King Show', ATV, U.K.
Fri 15 'Top Gear' Radio Programme, U.K.
Sat 16 'Top of the Pops', BBC-TV
Fri 22 'Christmas on Earth, Continued' at the Olympia, London (with The Who, Pink Floyd, Soft Machine etc)

1968

JANUARY

Thu 4 Lorensburg Cirkus, Gothenburg, Sweden (2 shows) (Jimi arrested for smashing up hotel room)
Fri 5 Jernallen Sports Hall, Sandvikan, Sweden (2 shows)
Sat 6 Swedish TV interviews
Sun 7 Falkoner Hall, Copenhagen, Denmark (2 shows)
Mon 8 Konserthus, Stockholm, Sweden (2 shows)
Fri 12 Jimi goes to court for smashing hotel room and must stay in Sweden another week
Sun 28 Pop Club, Paris
Mon 29 L'Olympia, Paris (with The Animals) (2 shows)
Tue 30 To U.S.A. for 2nd J.H.E. Tour
Wed 31 Press Conference, Pan Am Building, New York

FEBRUARY

Thu 1 Start of Tour 60 cities in 66 days! Fillmore West, San Francisco

Fri 2 Winterland, San Francisco (2 shows)
Sat 3 Winterland, San Francisco (2 shows)
Sun 4 Winterland, San Francisco
Mon 5 Tempe, Arizona
Tue 6 Tucson, Arizona
Thu 8 Sacramento, California
Fri 9 Convention Centre, Anaheim, California (2 shows)
Sat 10 Shrine Auditorium, Los Angeles
Sun 11 Santa Barbara, California
Mon 12 Centre Arena, Seattle, Washington
Tue 13 Jimi sees his family and old school for the first time in nearly 7 years
Wed 14 Denver, Colorado
Thu 15 Municipal Auditorium, San Antonio, Texas
Fri 16 Memorial Auditorium, Dallas, Texas
Sat 17 Will Rogers Auditorium, Ft. Worth, Texas
Sun 18 Houston, Texas (2 shows)
Wed 21 Electric Factory, Philadelphia (2 shows)
Thu 22 Electric Factory, Philadelphia (2 shows)
Fri 23 Masonic Hall, Detroit, Michigan
Sat 24 C.N.E. Coliseum, Toronto, Canada
Sun 25 Civic Opera House, Chicago
Tue 27 Madison, Wisconsin (2 shows)
Wed 28 Milwaukee, Wisconsin (2 shows)
Thu 29 Milwaukee, Wisconsin (2 shows)

MARCH

Sat 2 Hunter College, New York
Sun 3 Veterans Memorial Auditorium, Columbus, Ohio
Fri 8 Brown University, Providence, Rhode Island
Sat 9 Stony Brook, N.Y.U., Long Island, New York
Sun 10 Washington D.C. (2 shows)
Fri 15 Atwood Hall, Clark University, Worcester, Mass. (2 shows)
Sat 16 Lewiston, Maine
Sun 17 Cafe-A-Go-Go, New York (Jimi and Mitch)
Tue 19 Capitol Theatre, Ottowa, Canada (2 shows)
Thu 21 War Memorial, Rochester, N.Y.C.
Fri 22 Hartford, Conn.
Sat 23 Memorial Auditorium, Buffalo, N.Y.
Sun 23 Masonic Temple, Detroit, Michigan
Tue 26 Music Hall, Cleveland, Ohio
Wed 27 Muncie, Indiana
Thu 28 Xavier University, Cincinnati, Ohio
Fri 29 Illinois University Hall, Chicago (cancelled after 2 electric faults)
Sat 30 Fieldhouse, Toledo University, Ohio
Sun 31 Philadelphia, Pennsylvania

APRIL

Tue 2 Paul Suave Arena, Montreal, Quebec, Canada
Thu 4 Virginia Beach, Virginia (2 shows) (2nd show cancelled due to Martin Luther King's death and surrounding confusion)
Fri 5 Symphony Hall, Newark, New Jersey
Sat 6 White Plains Convention Center, New York
Fri 19 Rensselaer Polytechnic, Troy, N.Y.

MAY

Wed 1 to Thu 9 Recording Record Plant, N.Y.C.
Fri 10 Fillmore East, New York (with Sly and The Family Stone)
Sat 18 Miami Pop Festival, Miami, Florida (2nd show rained off)
Wed 22 J.H.E to Italy
Thu 23 Piper Club, Milan
Fri 24 Brancassio Theatre, Rome (2 shows)
Sat 25 Brancassio Theatre, Rome (2 shows)
Sun 26 Bologne, Italy
Mon 27 J.H.E. return to London

Wed 29 J.H.E. fly to Zurich, Switzerland
Thu 30 Beat Monster Concert, Hallenstadien, Zurich
Fri 31 Beat Monster Concert, Hallenstadien, Zurich

JUNE

Wed 5 Dusty Springfield TV Show, A.T.V.. London

JULY

Sat 6 Woburn Abbey Pop Festival, U.K.
          (only J.H.E. U.K. concert 1968)
Mon 15 Sgt. Pepper's Club, Majorca, Spain
Tue 30 Shreveport, Louisiana (2 shows)
Wed 31 Lakeshore Auditorium, Baton Rouge, Louisiana
          (2 shows)

AUGUST

Thu 1 City Park Stadium, New Orleans, Louisiana
Fri 2 San Antonio, Texas
Sat 3 Southern Methodist University, Dallas
Sun 4 Sam Houston Coliseum, Texas
Sat 10 Chicago, Illinois (2 shows)
Sun 11 Colonial Ballroom, Davenport, Iowa
Fri 16 Post Pavilion, Baltimore, Maryland
Sat 17 Municipal Auditorium, Atlanta, Georgia
          (2 shows)
Sun 18 Curtis Hixon Hall, nr. Tampa, Florida
Tue 20 The Mosque, Richmond, Virginia (2 shows)
Wed 21 Virginia Beach, Virginia
Fri 23 Singer Bowl, Flushing Meadow Park, N.Y.
Sat 24 Bushnell Memorial Hall, Hartford, Conn.
Sun 25 Carousel Theatre, Framingham, Mass.
Mon 26 Bridgeport, Connecticut
Fri 30 Opera House, Salt Lake City, Utah

SEPTEMBER

Sun 1 Denver, Colorado
Tue 3 Balboa Stadium, San Diego, California
Wed 4 Phoenix, Arizona
Thu 5 San Bernadino, California
Fri 6 Center Coliseum, Seattle, Washington
Sat 7 Pacific Coliseum, Vancouver, Canada
Sun 8 Spokane, Washington
Mon 9 Portland, Oregon
Fri 13 Oakland Coliseum, Oakland, California
Sat 14 Hollywood Bowl, Los Angeles
Sun 15 Sacramento, California

OCTOBER

Sat 5 International Center, Honolulu, Hawaii
Thu 10 Winterland, San Francisco, California
Fri 11 Winterland, San Francisco, California
Sat 12 Winterland, San Francisco, California
Sat 26 Bakersfield, California

NOVEMBER

Fri 1 Kansas City, Missouri
Sat 2 Minneapolis, Minnesota
Sun 3 St Louis, Missouri
Sat 16 Cincinnati, Ohio
Sun 17 Yale University, New Haven, Connecticut
Fri 22 Jacksonville, Florida
Sat 23 Tampa, Florida
Wed 27 Providence, Rhode Island
Thu 28 Philharmonic Hall, New York (2 shows)
Sat 30 Cobo Hall, Detroit, Michigan

DECEMBER

Sun 1 Coliseum, Chicago
Thu 12 Rock 'n' Roll Circus (Mitch, John Lennon, Eric
          Clapton and Keith Richards)

1969

JANUARY

Sat 4 "Lulu Show" BBC-TV, London
Wed 8 Lorensburg Cirkus, Gothenburg, Sweden
          (2 shows)
Thu 9 Konserthus, Stockholm, Sweden (2 shows)

Fri 10 Falkoner Theatre, Copenhagen, Denmark
          (2 shows)
Sat 11 Musikhalle, Hamburg, West Germany
          (2 shows)
Sun 12 Rheinhalle, Dusseldorf, W. Germany (2 shows)
Mon 13 Sporthalle, Koln, W. Germany
Tue 14 Halle Munsterland, Munster, W. Germany
Wed 15 Deutsches Museum, Munich, W. Germany
          (2 shows)
Thu 16 Meistersingerhalle, Nurnburg, W. Germany
          (2 shows)
Fri 17 Jahrhunderthalle, Frankfurt, W. Germany
          (2 shows)
Sun 19 Liederhalle, Stuttgart, W. Germany (2 shows)
Tue 21 Strasbourg, France
Wed 22 Konzerthaus, Vienna, Austria (2 shows)
Thu 23 Sportpalast, West Berlin, W. Germany

FEBRUARY

Tue 18 Royal Albert Hall, London (R.A. Hall were
          only U.K. concerts in 1969)
Mon 24 Royal Albert Hall, London

APRIL

Wed 9 Fly to U.S.A. for start Spring Tour
          (recording in between concert dates)
Fri 11 Dayton Arena, Raleigh, N.C.
Sat 12 Spectrum, Philadelphia, Pennsylvania
Fri 18 Mid-South Coliseum, Memphis, Tennessee
Sat 19 Sam Houston Auditorium, Houston, Texas
Sun 20 Memorial Auditorium, Dallas, Texas
Sat 26 Forum, Los Angeles, California
Sun 27 Oakland Coliseum, California

MAY

Fri 2 Cobo Hall, Detroit, Michigan
Sat 3 Maple Leaf Gardens, Toronto, Canada
          (Jimi busted at airport for drugs)
Sun 4 Memorial Auditorium, Syracuse, N.Y.
Wed 7 University of Alabama, Tuscaloosa, Alabama
Fri 9 Coliseum, Charlotte, N.C.
Sat 10 Civic Center, Charleston, West Virginia
Sun 11 State Fair, Grand Coliseum, Indianapolis,
          Indiana
Fri 16 Civic Center, Baltimore, M.D.
Sat 17 R.I. Auditorium, Providence, Rhode Island
Sun 18 Madison Square Gardens, New York
Fri 23 Center Coliseum, Seattle, Washington
Sat 24 Sports Arean, San Diego, California
Sun 25 Santa Clara Rock Festival, California
Fri 30 Waikiki Shell, Honolulu, Hawaii
          (show cancelled, electric fault)
Sat 31 Waikiki Shell, Honolulu, Hawaii

JUNE

Sun 1 Waikiki Shell, Honolulu, Hawaii
Fri 20 Newport Pop Festival, Devonshire Downs,
          California
Sun 29 Mile High Stadium, Denver, Colorado (last date
          of Tour and Noel's last concert with Jimi and
          Mitch)

AUGUST

Mon 18 Woodstock Festival, New York

SEPTEMBER

Fri 5 Street Festival, Harlem, New York City
Wed 10 Salvation Club, New York City
Tue 30 Jimi, Mitch, Billy and band on Dick Cavett TV
          show U.S.A.

DECEMBER

Wed 31 Fillmore East debut, Band of Gypsys, Jimi,
          Billy and Buddy Miles

1970

JANUARY

Thu 1 Fillmore East, N.Y.C. B.O.G. (2 shows)

Tue 6 Record Plant, New York
Wed 7 Record Plant, New York
Wed 28 Madison Sq. Gardens, N.Y. (2nd and last
          concert dates with B.O.G.)
          (Jimi walks off stage, second show)

APRIL

Sat 25 L.A. Forum, California

MAY

Fri 1 Milwaukee, Wisconsin
Sat 2 Dane County Coliseum, Madison, Wisconsin
Sun 3 St. Paul, Minnesota
Mon 4 Village Gate, New York
Fri 8 University of Oklahoma, Oklahoma
Sat 9 Will Rogers Auditorium, Fort Worth, Texas
Sun 10 San Antonio Arena, San Antonio, Texas
Sat 16 Temple Stadium, Philadelphia, Pennsylvania
Fri 22 Cincinnati, Ohio (cancelled)
Sat 23 Kiel Auditorium, St Louis, Mo.
Sun 24 Veterans Memorial Auditorium, Columbus,
          Ohio (2 shows)
Sat 30 Berkeley Community Theater, Berkeley,
          California

JUNE

Fri 5 Memorial Auditorium, Dallas, Texas
Sat 6 Sam Houston Coliseum, Houston, Texas
Sun 7 Assembly Center Arena, Tulsa, Oklahoma
Tue 9 Memphis, Tennessee
Wed 10 Evansville, Indiana
Sat 13 Baltimore Civic Center, Baltimore, MD.
Sun 14 Recording, N.Y.C.
to
Wed 17
Fri 19 Albequerque, New Mexico
Sat 20 Swing Auditorium, San Bernadino, California
Sun 21 Ventura County Playgrounds, Ventura,
          California
Tue 23 Monmouth Gardens, Denver, Colorado
Sat 27 Boston Gardens, Boston, Massachusetts

JULY

Sat 4 Atlanta Pop Festival, Gainsville, Georgia
Sun 5 Miami Hiali Fronton, Florida
Fri 17 Randalls Island Festival, Downing Stadium,
          New York
Sat 25 Sports Arena, San Diego, California
Sun 26 Sicks Stadium, Seattle, Washington
Thu 30 Magical Gardens, Mauii, Hawaii

AUGUST

Sat 1 Honolulu International Centre, Oahu, Hawaii
Fri 14 Opening Electric Lady Studios, N.Y.
Sun 30 Isle of Wight Festival, East Afton Farm, IoW,
          U.K.
Mon 31 Gröna Lund, Stockholm, Sweden

SEPTEMBER

Tue 1 Liseburg, Gothenburg, Sweden
Wed 2 Vejlby Risskov Hall, Aarhus, Denmark
Thu 3 K.B. Hallen, Copenhagen, Denmark
Fri 4 Deutschlandhalle, Berlin, W. Germany
Sat 5 Isle of Fehmarn, W. Germany
          (cancelled)
Sun 6 Isle of Fehmarn, W. Germany
          (last concert of Jimi's)
Mon 7 Billy ill, all return to London, rest of tour
          cancelled
Thu 17 Jimi to meet Mitch and Sly Stone at the
          Speakeasy in London, for a jam – but never
          turned up.
Fri 18 11.25 am, Jimi pronounced dead at St. Mary
          Abbots Hospital, Kensington

OCTOBER

Thu 1 Jimi buried in Seattle, U.S.A, Greenwood
          Cemetery

INDEX